The Liners

of

Liverpool

by

Derek M. Whale

Part III

Cover Design: ERIC R. MONKS

First published 1988 by Countyvise Limited, 1 & 3 Grove Road, Rock Ferry, Birkenhead, Wirral, Merseyside L42 3XS.

Copyright © Derek M. Whale, 1988.
Photoset and printed by Birkenhead Press Limited, 1 & 3 Grove Road, Rock Ferry, Birkenhead, Merseyside L42 3XS.

ISBN 0 907768 12 1.

Index

Acknowledgements

I thank all the copyright holders of photographs and illustrations in these books — especially the Liverpool Daily Post & Echo (whose pictures are acknowledged as D.P. & E.). And all those whom it has not been possible to trace.

My thanks also to the following for their most helpful assistance: Anchor Line (Mr. William Higgins); Bibby Line (Mr. Derek Bibby, M.C. Chairman); Booth Line and Lamport and Holt (Mr. Denis Ormesher); Canadia Pacific Public Relations Department (Miss Amanda Pollard and Mr. Peter Alhadeff); Mr. Craig Carter; Mr. Allan S. Clayton; Mr. John Crowley; Cunard Archives, University of Liverpool (Mr. Michael Cook and Miss Andrea Rudd); Furness Withy Group P.R. Department (Mr. Richard Alexander); Captain Harry M. Hignett; Merseyside Maritime Museum (Mr. Michael Stammers); Mr. Eric Munday; Ocean Transport and Trading (Miss Sally Furlong and Miss Jenny Lovatt); Pacific Steam Navigation Company (Mr. John Lingwood); Mr. Reginald Page; Mr. John Partington; Mr. Mike Sheehan — and my daughter, Helen Jane.

For those who may not yet have read Part II of The Liners of Liverpool, here is the list of ships which this contains:—
Athenia, Berengaria, Britannic (I), (II) and (III), Caledonia, Ceramic, Cilicia, Circassia (II), the Empresses of: Australia (I), Britain (I) (Montroyal), Britain (II), Britain (III) (Queen Anna Maria/Carnivale), Canada (I), Canada (II) (ex-Duchess of Richmond), Canada (III) (Mardi Gras), England (Ocean Monarch), France (ex-Duchess of Bedford) and Russia. Also, the Georgic, Letitia (Empire Brent/Captain Cook), and some little anecdotes about sea-cats.

Foreword

by Michael Stammers
Assistant Director, Merseyside Maritime Museum

The great liners were so much part of the life of the port and the city of Liverpool that it is still hard to believe they have gone forever. Perhaps we almost took it for granted that there would always be a Cunarder or a Canadian Pacific ship tied up along the Landing Stage, busy with tugs, taxis and boat-trains.

Now, the whole scene has been transformed; the last liner sailed over a decade ago, the beloved Landing Stage has been sold for scrap and the famous Riverside Station, terminus of the boat-trains, stands derelict without its roof.

But though the last of the liners has gone, the people of Merseyside have not forgotten them. Indeed, many served aboard them and many more have watched their arrival and departure.

There are few Merseysiders without at least one relative, friend or ancestor who went to sea in the liners. So there are memories, many memories. Derek Whale has written not just a history of the ships but also recorded in print for future generations the stories, thoughts and feelings of the people who knew and sailed the liners.

It is as vital to preserve the oral history of our maritime heritage as it is to preserve the models, pictures, photographs and plans of the ships. I hope that Derek Whale will continue with more stories from the people of Merseyside's liner era.

Introduction

Here is the last of the trio of parts to complete The Liners of Liverpool.

This book has become not just a local best-seller but one which already has found its way to many parts of Britain and Ireland and to countries like Australia, South America, the U.S.A. and Canada.

Part III includes the former Cunard "quadruplets" — Saxonia, Ivernia, Carinthia and Sylvania — en bloc, as these were almost identical sisters, all built between 1954 and 1957.

I have dealt with some of the "shire" liners, like the Oxfordshire and the Devonshire, in a similar manner.

As Elder Dempster's flagship, the Aureol, was the last regular big passenger liner to leave Liverpool, I thought it fitting that, in this final part, the curtain should ring down on that scene!

The Aba, Apapa and Accra also are contained in the last chapters.

Some readers, obviously, will be disappointed that certain ships — perhaps those in which they or their relatives or friends once served — have not been mentioned.

But, in writing a relatively short book of this nature, I could not possibly include all the names in the long fleet lists of the big liner companies, giving their histories and interesting exploits.

For this reason, I have simply selected some of those whose names are better known to the layman, and to give some examples of the great ships of yesteryear — in particular for the benefit of the younger generation which never saw them.

Here and there, throughout the three parts of the book, are recorded instances of great hardship and courage by officers and crews, especially in time of war.

There literally were thousands of these incidents in the wars at sea and I regret that I have been unable to record more within the scope of this book.

CUNARD'S FAMOUS QUADS

Saxonia, Ivernia, Carinthia and Sylvania

This is the tale of four lovely sisters — Cunard's bonny 22,000-ton quadruplets, Saxonia, Ivernia, Carinthia and Sylvania.

They were built between 1954 and 1957, especially for service to Quebec and Montreal, and were the largest the company ever constructed for that purpose. All were products of the famous John Brown's shipyard on Clydeside — the birthplace of the giants Queen Mary and Queen Elizabeth — their shallow draft and short masts enabling them to pass under the St. Lawrence bridges. And each carried a stern anchor for the St. Lawrence River.

All of them differed considerably from the older type of passenger liners, which often had high 'tween-deck spaces — like the Empress of Scotland, for example, one of whose rooms rose through two decks and even boasted a musicians' gallery. So the lower 'tween-deck spaces and the interesting variety of smaller rooms in the new "quads" were particularly noticeable at the time they were built.

They all bore the same profile and dimensions and, to the casual observer, looked alike, although Ivernia had square portholes below her bridge. But even as human quads have their own respective characters, so did this sparkling quartette. Their interior designs and decorations, for instance, were each unique and, of course, they created their own distinctive histories as they ploughed their various paths across the high seas.

Passengers, officers and crews will always remember them for their particular characteristics, voyages and numerous events, good and bad, which moulded their interesting careers.

Saxonia

Lady Churchill, wife of Sir Winston Churchill, named the £5 million Saxonia at the launching ceremony on February 17, 1954. Saxonia could carry 125 first-class passengers and 800 tourist class. She had 300,000 cubic feet capacity for cargo. She boasted a tiered cinema and three attractive lounges, called the Crystal, the Chintz and the Garden, the latter looking rather like a Parisian terrace cafe, with flowers. The influence of modern Canada was reflected in her restaurants — the Maple Leaf and the Odahmin. Some of the upholstery reproduced the patterns of Indian tribal blankets and the shirts of Yukon gold miners.

Saxonia arrived in the Mersey on August 23, 1954, sporting a dome-top funnel — a new style for Cunarders, fashioned to lessen smoke-drift over the upper decks.

With Captain Andrew MacKellar in command, she made her maiden voyage from Liverpool to Quebec and Montreal on Thursday, September 2, her passengers including several hundred

Saxonia nearing completion on the Clyde, in early August, 1954, shortly before moving into dry dock for the finishing touches.
(John Brown (Clydebank) Ltd.)

emigrants. This was a joyful occasion and in complete contrast to the sad Merseyside spectacle only the day before, when the fire-gutted hulk of the famous Empress of Canada was towed away for breaking up. The old Cunard liner, Ascania, (often irreverently called the 'Ashcan' by some of her crew), saluted Saxonia, and with messages of goodwill, including those from Sir Ivan Thompson, Commodore of the Cunard fleet, and the Queen Mary, she sped on her way.

Saxonia proved her worth. On that first voyage of 5 days, 2 hours and 12 minutes from the Bar Lightship at Liverpool to Father Point, Canada, she steamed at an average speed of 20.04 knots to lower the sailing times for comparable ships of the same line on the Mersey-St. Lawrence run. On her return, she beat their shortest time for the crossing from Father Point to the Mersey Bar (5 days, 5 hours) by

8

reaching the Bar in 4 days, 23 hours, 24 minutes — in spite of three days of gales and stopping to shelter in Anglesey's Moelfre Bay.

I remember standing on the old wooden Liverpool landing stage on September 5, 1956, watching the Saxonia in mid-river. When weighing her port-bow anchor, she hauled up a rusty, 9-ton anchor with her own. The latter was found to have belonged to another Cunarder — the ill-fated liner, Lancastria, which lost it in 1924.

With the completion of the Ivernia in June, 1955, plans were made for the two sisters to be transferred from the Mersey to Southampton. They were to sail from there to Canada, via Le Havre, to tap the Continental tourist trade. The other sisters, Carinthia and Sylvania, would maintain the passenger service from Liverpool to Canada.

Saxonia made her first voyage from London on January 31, 1958. She joined Ivernia in operating Cunard's off-season schedules from London to Halifax, Nova Scotia and New York.

Both sisters underwent a £2 million conversion to cruise liners at John Brown's yard during the winter of 1962/63. They were also renamed. Saxonia became the Carmania, and Ivernia the Franconia. These names belonged to former well-known Cunarders. Saxonia inherited a very honourable name as the original Carmania which wrote a fine page in maritime history as the auxiliary cruiser that sank the Cap Trafalgar, the heavily-armed German auxiliary cruiser, in the South Atlantic in September, 1914.

Mention of the Great War brings to mind a very interesting but probably long-forgotten story about the crew of the original (1900) Saxonia.

It concerned a group of influential Merseyside businessmen actually providing a supper, binge and even mementoes for a group of seafaring strikers!

This took place at Liverpool's famous old restaurant, the Bear's Paw, on December 10, 1915.

The strikers were members of Saxonia's crew, who had walked ashore, when 800 young male passengers boarded the ship hoping to sail overseas and miss the 1914-18 War call-up!

Saxonia's 'strikers' refused to assist them evade this duty.

A whip-round among the hosts raised £70 for the seamen, each of whom was also given a red, white and blue box containing a silver-mounted pipe and a pouch of tobacco.

The newly-named liners were each prepared for Cunard's new Canadian summer service from Rotterdam, via Southampton, Le Havre and Cobh, to Quebec and Montreal. Carmania was first to complete her refit and began the service in April, 1963. She was

R.M.S. Saxonia before her name-change.   (Cunard Line)

joined by Franconia in the June. In November, that year, both ships left Southampton for the winter dollar-earning cruising season. Carmania was based at Fort Lauderdale, in Florida, and Franconia in New York. In April, 1964, both liners returned to Southampton for the summer Canadian service.

They were provided with night clubs, teenagers' rooms, complete with juke box and bowling alleys. Hatches, holds and cargo gear were ripped out to produce kidney-shaped swimming pools, nearly as large as the Queen Mary's first-class pool, plus paddling pools for small children. Forty-foot long buffet serveries were constructed for the provision of hot and cold lunches for passengers wishing to remain on deck. Both of the vessels' hulls and superstructures were painted in the shades of green until then exclusive to the Cunard cruise liner, Caronia, but still retaining their black-topped red funnels.

All this sounded wonderful, but Carmania and Franconia were not returning to the Mersey with their new looks. With more and more folk flying across the North Atlantic, together with intense competition from foreign shipping, British liner companies were having to seriously appraise their passenger fleets. Only the Sylvania and the Carinthia were then using Liverpool, where, not so long before, there had been five Cunarders operating from that port. As a Liverpool steamship owner put it at that time: "It is regrettable, but Liverpool's liner trade appears to be fading. Now, efforts are being concentrated on cargoes."

Captain William James Law, 53, commanded the Carmania. He had been master of the ship when she was known as the Saxonia.

A love-hate relationship has long existed between ships' crews and dockers, irrespective of the so-called fraternity among the unions.

Carmania briefly was caught up between these two factions in October, 1963, when 3,800 members of the International Longshoremen's Association walked off their jobs in the St. Lawrence River ports over a demand for higher wages. Striking dockers pelted the Carmania in a half-hour battle at Quebec, as she prepared to sail to Southampton with 300 passengers. Stones and coins were hurled by the dockers and Carmania's crew turned fire hoses on them!

Carmania made her first cruise from Britain in Cunard's 1966-67 programme, on October 1, 1966. This was an autumn sunshine cruise from Southampton to Gibraltar, Villafranche, Naples and Palma. Carinthia made her 14-day Christmas cruise from Liverpool, taking

All decked out to go cruising – Carmania in 1963.   (Cunard Line)

in Madeira, Tenerife, Las Palmas, Gibraltar and Lisbon. Highlight of the company's programme was a new West Indies cruise by the Sylvania, sailing from Southampton on January 13, 1967.

April that year saw, for the first time, four Cunarders being used as floating hotels while in port in Canada. Visitors to the Expo 67 Exhibition in Montreal — Canada's giant World's Fair — were able to live on board Carmania, Sylvania and Carinthia. Cunard were cashing in on the tourist boom.

Even Franconia came off her weekly New York to Bermuda service, bringing passengers to Montreal to visit the exhibition.

Franconia then made a 12-day cruise, calling at Quebec, Boston, Bermuda, Charlottetown, Prince Edward Island, and the French island of St. Pierre et Miquelon, before returning to her Bermuda run.

Post-war cruising introduced some new titles for certain members of a liner's complement — like that of hotel manager which, somehow, seems to be infra dig in maritime parlance! And yet, this was a very apt title because the officer appointed was indeed in charge of a floating hotel — and, with the big companies, these were in the five-star category. The job involved responsibility of catering for, perhaps, a thousand or more passengers, 24 hours a day; not to mention the high percentage of epicures who are always to be found on liners. And the title "entertainments director" on cruise liners speaks for itself! Anyone who has had experience of arranging functions, however large or small, glamorous or mundane, knows only too well what headaches these can be. A question of big fish and little fish, maybe, but organising entertainment on the world's big cruise liners with something to please a wide variety of tastes, for the duration of the voyage, must be a nail-biting exercise for the directors of entertainment.

So, when the American authorities suddenly cancelled the 15-day Caribbean Christmas cruise arranged for the Carmania out of Port Everglades, Florida, with 450 passengers, in September, 1968, there must have been many very worried Cunard staff. The cancellation, said Cunard, was over the refusal to accept the liner's Board of Trade Certificate under "a new interpretation by United States Government authorities on international regulations on safety at sea."

With its time-honoured peacetime safety record, Cunard had suffered a great slight. The "new interpretation" also heralded a serious implication for British shipping generally. Sir Basil Smallpeice, Cunard's chairman, declared that the U.S. action was a breach of an undertaking given by the U.S. Secretary of State to the British Embassy in Washington earlier that year.

The trouble was caused by the U.S. Coast Guard at Miami complaining about an alleged fire risk with the entrance doors to the first-class restaurant in Carmania. Cunard had been told about this only two days before the ban, giving the company insufficient time to carry out the necessary work before the sailing date. Not least of this slight to Britain was its obvious shattering effect on the country's national pride. After all, Britain had pioneered safety at sea!

Sir Basil said: "This is the first time in history, so far as I am aware, that a Board of Trade Certificate has been overruled by any authority, in the United States or anywhere else!"

However, in spite of the dispute, the Coast Guard permitted the Carmania to leave on her cruise. But Lady Luck was in no mood to

Carmania. She ran around "from bow to bridge" on a Bahamas cruise in January, 1969. (Cunard Line)

smile on Carmania (Captain Maurice Hehir), which ran aground from bow to bridge on the coral sand of San Salvador Island, in the Bahamas, on January 12, 1969. She was like a giant whale on the Gardener Reef, 300 miles from Nassau.

With typical British sang froid, Staff Captain Peter Jackson reported: "The situation on board is quite normal." In fact, the drama had only added to the excitement and festivity on the liner, with passengers dancing and singing on the decks — in spite of temperatures in the 80's. The stranding had its historical touch, too. San Salvador was the first landfall of Christopher Columbus in 1492, in his quest for the New World. It is to the credit of Cunard that even 48 hours after the stranding, Captain Jackson was able to say: "So far, no one is complaining. We have not yet had demands for disembarkation." Still, even the best-tempered folk have to draw the line somewhere and, later, some of the passengers began to feel a bit ruffled.

After some vain attempts by tugs to pull Carmania off the sandbank, it was announced that the 15,400-ton Italian liner, Flavia (coincidentally, the former popular little Cunarder, Media), came to the rescue and took on board Carmania's passengers and up to 150 of her crew. The fifth attempt to free the liner by three ocean-going tugs was successful after thousands of tons of fresh water and fuel oil had been discharged. She had been trapped for six days and she sailed to Newport News, U.S.A., for a full inspection and repairs.

Cunard's private inquiry into this mishap revealed that the Admiralty chart of that area was inaccurate and showed between 20 and 60 fathoms at the spot where the Carmania grounded. A company spokesman, however, said the inquiry had also concluded that there had been some error of judgement on the part of the acting master of the ship, Captain Hehir, who suffered loss of seniority and reverted to the rank of Chief Officer. Captain Hehir's previous record in command was said to have been "one of outstanding seamanship and that his bearing and handling of the Carmania after she went aground was exemplary."

Troubles, it is said, never come singly, and only a few months later, in May, Carmania was in collision with the 8,000-ton Russian tanker, Frunze, shortly after leaving Gibraltar with 644 passsengers. Carmania's starboard bow plating was damaged.

Famous businessman Sir Basil Smallpeice pictured (centre) before the Cunard Steam-Ship Company's annual meeting in June, 1966. He is accompanied by the deputy chairman, Mr. Ronald H. Senior (left) and Mr. Anthony H. Hume.
(D.P. & E.)

Ivernia

More than two months before Saxonia was launched, Ivernia's name was "booked". It happened like this:—

In 1900, Cunard built two sister ships, also called the Saxonia and the Ivernia, so when the company was building the new 22,000-ton sister to its latest liner, the Saxonia, naturally it was hoped to retain the other original name. But it was discovered that this name was already taken. It belonged to a 50-ton private yacht, owned by Mr. and Mrs. Leslie Boyd, and was moored in the Thames at Richmond!

The Cunard Steam-Ship Company asked the Boyds if they would permit the name of their vessel to be transferred to the new liner — then just humble Number 693 in John Brown's shipyard on the Clyde. Although the couple knew that it was supposed to be unlucky to change the name of a boat they also appreciated that their yacht had already undergone a name-change, anyway. So, they agreed and then had the awesome task of finding another name for their yacht — different from the 37,000 which were then already registered. They chose Leiden. Cunard not only offered to pay all the costs involved in the change-over (Ivernia was on the name-plates, bell, dinghy and even printed on the linen!) but also to show the Boyds' two children over the Queen Mary.

Ivernia, with the same overall dimensions as the Saxonia (608 feet long and 80 feet wide), was duly launched on December 14, 1954 — in a gale and assisted by five tugs. Fittingly for a ship destined for the Canadian service, she was named by Mrs. Clarence Howe, wife of the Canadian Minister of Trade and Commerce. Like Saxonia, the liner's interior decoration also showed her close relationship with Canada. Her tourist smokers' room displayed numerous murals, consisting of a series of specially-commissioned paintings, linking towns in Britain with their namesakes in Canada. The first-class cocktail bar was called the Mounties' Bar, inspired by the life and work of the Canadian Mounted Police.

Ivernia cost £5 million and was the second of the quartette. Soon after her launching, the keel of the third sister, Carinthia, was laid, although at that time she was known simply as Number 699. Among the messages of goodwill read out at the ceremony lunch was a telegram reading: "Best of luck to you and all who sail in you. From your Godmother — Leiden, ex-Ivernia."

So many famous ships had made their maiden voyages from Liverpool that it came as quite a surprise to learn that Cunard had decided Ivernia should make her maiden voyage on July 1, 1955, sailing direct from Greenock to Quebec and Montreal. Because of the current dock strike, however, arrangements for a special-guest running-in cruise had to be cancelled and the new ship lay in the

The new Ivernia on her arrival at Liverpool for the first time – July 19, 1955. The "White Empress" on the right is Canadian Pacific's Empress of France.
(D.P. &. E.)

quietude of Scotland's Gare Loch, with famous Royal Navy warships, like the King George V and the aircraft-carrier, Illustrious, to keep her company.

After her trials, Ivernia, tied up at the breaker's yard in Faslane, Gare Loch, to take on stores. Thus, she went from "the makers to the breakers" before her maiden voyage!

Her passengers, who should have embarked at Liverpool, and many of whom came from as far as London, travelled to Scotland by special train and were taken out to the liner, anchored in the Clyde, by tender. In sailing from the Clyde, with Captain A.B. Fasting in command, Ivernia followed in the wake of the Queen Elizabeth, which sailed from that river on her secret, wartime maiden voyage, in March, 1940, and she was the only other Cunarder up to then to have done so.

Sadly, for once, maritime-orientated Merseyside did not give Ivernia the welcome-home that she deserved after her quiet retreat from the Clyde to Canada. Dressed overall, carrying 942 passengers and appearing for the first time in the Mersey on July 19, she received but few toots of welcome from the local shipping. (Not that there was much around then!). She had made the outward passage in 4 days, 17 hours, 16 minutes, and returned in 4 days, 19 hours, 47 minutes, at an average speed of 21.04 knots over the longer route from Montreal to Liverpool. This was faster than Saxonia's maiden voyage times. However, a large party of Cunard's guests gave Ivernia an appreciative once-over when they toured the ship as she lay in Huskisson Dock, Liverpool, on July 25.

Ivernia played Santa Claus that maiden-voyage year by bringing to Liverpool 74 wives and children of some members of the Canadian forces in Germany. They disembarked and were taken by coach to Manchester Airport for their flight to Dusseldorf.

Autumn, 1956, saw further changes in Cunard's programme, when it planned to send Ivernia and Saxonia to Southampton for service to the U.S. and Canada. This would leave the new Carinthia and the Sylvania — the fourth and final sister of the fabulous quartette — operating out of Liverpool. Sylvania was due to make her maiden voyage in June, 1957. Ivernia's first runs before going to Southampton were from London to Halifax, Nova Scotia, and New York via Le Havre. She became the first Cunard passenger liner to sail from London since 1952, when the 20,000-ton Scythia made several voyages from the capital to Canada.

This new Liverpool liner kept herself in the news while operating from Southampton. In April, 1957, she was given the job of ferrying passengers from the Queen Mary, berthed at Cherbourg, to Plymouth. The Queen Mary had arrived at the French port with more than a thousand passengers but was blacklisted by dockers in her home port of Southampton. While she remained in France with her crew, preparing to turn round for New York again, Ivernia was dispatched to carry the Queen's arriving and departing passengers across the Channel.

Outward-bound for Montreal, on April 25, 1961, Ivernia grounded on a mudbank shortly after leaving Southampton. It took nine tugs to free her and she was delayed for some 19 hours.

This picture shows Ivernia as the backcloth to a tragic scene. In the foreground of the liner as she moves down river in November, 1955, a salvage operation is under way to beach the coaster, Bannprince, which sank twelve days earlier with the loss of one life. (Medley and Bird, Wallasey)

Ivernia (like the Saxonia) was renamed in the autumn of 1962. She became know as Franconia, after two previous ships of that name. Considerable alterations (costing a million pounds for each ship) at John Brown's Clydebank shipyard, were made to Ivernia and Saxonia, as mentioned in the last chapter. The alterations also included those to the passenger accommodation, providing all first-class staterooms and the majority of tourist-class staterooms with their own private bath or shower and lavatory. New fuel and fresh water tanks extended the sister liners' range for cruising and each also was equipped with four large cruise launches.

Both liners, as I have explained, were painted in the shades of pale green which, until then, were exclusive to the company's special cruise liner, Caronia. And because it seems shameful to omit mention of this latter lovely ship, I shall digress just briefly to outline her career . . . .

The 34,183-ton Caronia, known as the Green Goddess from her livery, was a beautiful ship, which must have been seen in most of the world's major ports. She was Cunard's luxurious premier cruise liner in her day and was launched by Princess Elizabeth in 1947, sailing on her maiden voyage from Southampton to New York on January 4, 1949. Caronia ended her Cunard service in November, 1967. She was to have become a floating hotel in a Yugoslavian port, but the deal fell through and she was sold in 1968 to the Franchard Corporation of New York, who set up the Star Shipping Company, S.A., of Panama, to operate exclusively on cruises out of U.S. ports.

High, wide and handsome – Caronia looks sternly at the camera as she undergoes her annual overhaul in Gladstone Graving Dock.
(Clayton Photos)

The liner at first was renamed Columbia, but this was changed to Caribia. After remaining idle at New York from March 25, 1969, she was sold in January, 1974, for breaking up in Taiwan. Caribia, however, died a nobler death. In the August, she had to be cut loose from her towing tug in a storm and ran aground at the entrance to Guam's Apra harbour. She partly sank and broke into three sections, causing a big headache over wreckage clearance, not to mention insurance!

My vivid memory of this fine ship is rather unusual in that, when visiting her in dock at Liverpool, I was permitted, with a photographer, to climb up the vertical ladder *within* her towering tubular mast right up to the crow's nest, from which the empty dock bottom seemed very far below! This took place when Caronia, as she was then still known, was undergoing a three-month overhaul, with

There's nothing like a cruise for meeting people from all walks of life, and a former Cunard head waiter, Mr. A. Forrest, from Liverpool, once told how several American gangsters enjoyed a cruise in the Caronia. "We had to make sure that they were seated at a single table with their bodyguard," he said .... Anything to please the customers!

It was wet and windy on Merseyside this January day in 1957, but the Caronia, preparing to leave Prince's Landing Stage, was soon to enjoy the sunshine of her 34,000-mile dollar-earning world cruise.
(D.P. & E.)

19

extensions to her air-conditioning, in Gladstone Graving Dock, in the winter of 1956 . . . .

The Carmania returned to service in April, 1963, and the Franconia, in the June, under the command of Captain R.J.N. Nicholas, of Wallasey, Merseyside.

In readiness for two 13-day cruises from Southampton to Spain and France in September and October, 1965, Franconia's sun lounge was converted into a casino, where passengers were able to gamble on blackjack and roulette, as well as traditional tombola. Cunard's decision to install these more sophisticated forms of gambling was taken at company top level. Seven croupiers were engaged. Following these successful cruises, sister Carmania was scheduled to make her first cruise from Britain in October the next year. That was a Mediterranean cruise. Meanwhile, between December, 1965 and April, 1966, Carmania was due to make nine West Indies cruises from Port Everglades, Florida.

During their overhauls in November, 1966, Carmania and Franconia lost their green cruising colour and were painted white. Carmania sailed to Miami, Florida, to start her dollar cruises. Franconia, sailing for New York, via Halifax, hit rough weather and by the time she arrived at New York her hull had returned to green again! She made two cruises from New York and then went south to join Carmania at Miami, where she made a further eight West Indies' cruises. In April, 1967, she went back to New York and took on the weekly Bermuda cruises — a role vacated by the Queen of Bermuda in November, 1966.

After nearly two years' absence, the Franconia returned to Liverpool to make her first-ever cruise out of that port — to Tangier, Madeira, Las Palmas, Casablanca, Gibraltar. Early in the following New Year, she made a second cruise from her old home port — to Lisbon, Madeira, Las Palmas, Casablanca, Gibraltar and back. For the majority of the liner's 700 passengers on the earlier cruise, it was their first Christmas Day afloat. Handling the tough job of planning a variety of entertainments for toddlers to adults was dancer Sheila Holt and Terry Conroy, at 28 then the youngest cruise entertainments director in the fleet. One form of "entertainment" unscheduled, but which certainly thrilled the passengers on that cruise, was the real-life drama performed by Franconia's master, 57-year-old Captain Phil Reade.

Told that there was a leak in the starboard propeller gland, Captain Reade, a native of Gosforth, Newcastle-on-Tyne, decided to do the job himself as the ship was at Tangier and it being the Moslem Feast of Ramadan, it would prove difficult to get repairs done. An experienced skin-diver, Captain Reade, assisted by senior mechanic, Kenneth King, of Parkgate, Southampton, made the shaft watertight with rope and plastic wrappings, within 55 minutes of their one hour's air supply. After the engineers had replaced the gland, the two men dived again to remove the wrappings and Franconia left on schedule for Madeira.

A few weeks later, at the end of January, 1968, Franconia left Liverpool on her 11-month tour as a dollar-earning liner on a regular

It was a bit like old times when Franconia returned to Liverpool Landing Stage on November 29, 1967. The liner, which once sailed regularly from the port, arrived after nearly two years' absence for her annual overhaul and to make her first cruise from Liverpool. (Gordon Whiting)

service between New York and Bermuda. On the first of those cruises out of New York she was involved in a rescue in the stormy Atlantic, having picked up an S.O.S. from the 15,797-ton Liberian steam tanker, Pegasos, 245 miles east of Cape Hatteras. The liner changed course and sped to aid the stricken vessel, lying low in a heavy swell, with 20ft. waves breaking over her. Another Liberian freighter took on board several men in a lifeboat and the U.S. aircraft carrier, Wasp, sent up her helicopters. These took off 13 men and a woman, the wife of the chief steward, and landed them on the deck of the Franconia, which carried them on to Bermuda. The captain of the Pegasos and five of the crew stayed with the ship.

In August, the same year, Franconia aided a 90ft. schooner in danger of sinking in the Atlantic, 300 miles off New York. She took on board five women and two children, while the men remained with

Her Blue Peter flying, Franconia is set fair to leave Liverpool on January 27, 1968, as a dollar-earning cruise liner between New York and Bermuda.
(D.P. & E.)

the ship. Indeed, this life-saving luxury liner ended her last voyage in Cunard's service by going to the rescue once again. She docked at Southampton on October 17, 1971, with eight members of the 12,000-ton fire-damaged Norwegian bulk carrier, Anatina. Franconia, returning with a skeleton crew from Florida, where she had been operating the New York-Bermuda run, was the first vessel to sight the Anatina, which was about 150 miles from Lands End, with flames coming from her wheelhouse. Lieut. Commander Harry Dormer, Franconia's chief officer, and four of her crew, led the rescue in a launch from the liner. Two of Anatina's crew died in the fire.

The end of October, 1971, saw Franconia and her sister, Carmania, laid up at Southampton, with a big question mark hanging over their future. The lovely 17-year-old sisters had both lost money that year — wiping out the profit made by the QE2 the year before. It was not long before action on their future was irrevocably taken. In December, Cunard decided to sell both ships because, said the company, it could not reach agreement with the National Union of Seamen on new manning requirements. Mr. Victor Matthews, the company chairman, said: "Without concessions from the union, it would prove impossible to run these older ships successfully in the highly competitive international cruise market."

After weeks of speculation, it was eventually confirmed by Cunard, in December, 1971, that it was selling the two liners. The asking price was £2 million. Meanwhile, both liners were laid up in the River Fal, in Cornwall. Finally, in August, 1973, Cunard signed

Summer skies smile on Franconia, in cruising mood at Hamilton, Bermuda.

an agreement to sell them to the Nikreis Maritime Corporation, of Panama City, an affiliate of Robin International, of New York, for about £1 million each. They changed hands after being surveyed at Tyneside and were then handed over to Russia, through Nickreis Maritime acting as agents for the State-owned Sovinflot.

The ships were renamed once more — each after a Russian singer. Carmania became Leonid Sobinov (the tenor), now operated by the U.S.S.R. Black Sea Shipping Company, of Odessa, and Franconia, Fyodor Shalyapin (the baritone), operating under the flag of the U.S.S.R. Far Eastern Steamship Company of Vladivostock.

Fyodor Shalyapin was to be based in Australia and she sailed there from Southampton in November, 1973. Leonid Sobinov followed in February, the next year to operate a passenger service between the U.K. and Australia.

A fascinating story concerns the Fyodor Shalyapin, when under charter for Shaw Savill Cruises of Australia, in 1976.

When sailing across the Tasman Sea, early one morning in darkness, she stopped and all her lights were extinguished. Passengers heard metallic noises and the ship's cranes were operated. A submarine came alongside and witnesses saw goods and personnel transformed to the sub and vice versa.

Franconia and Carmania laid up in the picturesque River Fal, Cornwall, in 1972, awaiting a buyer. On the right is the Shaw Savill liner, Southern Cross, which was sold to a Greek company and renamed Calypso.

The mystery deepened at Sydney, where both the Russian Embassy and Shaw Savill denied this incident — but 200 passengers who signed a letter to the Australian press reckoned that they knew better!

Both liners were banned, with other Soviet passenger ships, from operating from Australia, following the invasion of Afghanistan.

Fyodor Shalyapin (ex-Franconia) leaving the Tyne after her overhaul in November, 1973, bound for Riga, Latvia, where she took on a full crew and stores.

The original Carmania, which fought an incredible World War 1 battle with the German ship Cap Trafalgar in the south Atlantic. Both former luxury liners, they were heavily armed and disguised as each other!

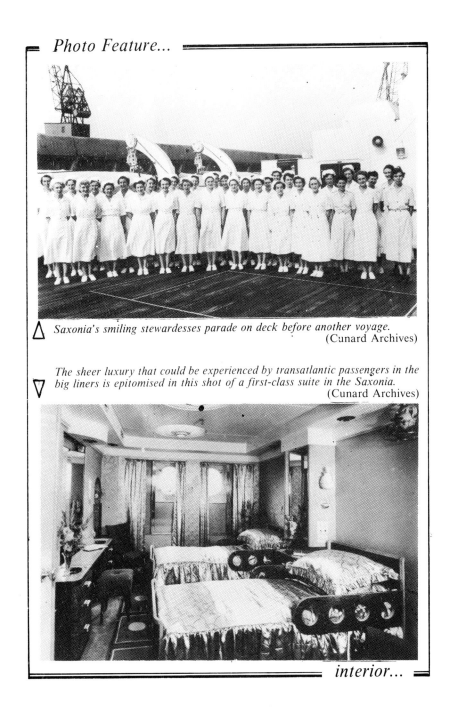

△ *Saxonia's smiling stewardesses parade on deck before another voyage.*
(Cunard Archives)

The sheer luxury that could be experienced by transatlantic passengers in the
▽ *big liners is epitomised in this shot of a first-class suite in the Saxonia.*
(Cunard Archives)

interior...

△ *A liner's kitchen can be the busiest place in a ship when hundreds of passengers must be fed – many times a day! Here are some of Saxonia's chefs at work among an impressive display of gleaming stainless-steel equipment.*
(Cunard Line Archives)

▽ *Part of Saxonia's splendid, air-conditioned tourist restaurant, which extended the full width of the ship.* (Cunard Archives)

Carmania's lido deck, brightly lit and so inviting on tropical cruises.
(Cunard Line)

△ *Ivernia's tourist smoking-room was a large, comfortable room incorporating a cheerfully fitted cocktail bar. Its "City Cousins" theme depicted cities and towns in Britain and their namesakes in Canada.* (Cunard Archives)

▽ *Countless letters and picture-postcards were written in Ivernia's neat little writing room.* (Cunard Archives)

interior... =

△ *Ivernia's Mounties' Bar honoured the Royal Canadian Mounted Police. Giant sergeants' chevrons imparted a novel design to the flooring.*(Cunard Archives)

▽ *The serenity and beauty of plants could be found in Ivernia's garden lounge – even way out on the wild North Atlantic!*

interior...

The suitably-furnished first-class sun lounge in Ivernia.

△ *Padded deck-chairs were among the passenger comforts of Carinthia's tourist class promenade deck.* (Cunard Archives)

▽ *The first-class smoking-room in Carinthia recalled the days of Tudor England.* (Cunard Line)

interior...

△ *Decoration in the French rococo style lent grace and sophistication to Carinthia's first-class restaurant.* (Cunard Archives)

▽ *The central circular area of Carinthia's elegant first-class lounge, and the piano, right, gave room and atmosphere for dancing.* (Cunard Archives)

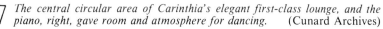

interior...

Cheerful chef, George Woodward, arranging part of a mouth-watering display of seasonal fare in the Sylvania for the liner's voyage from Liverpool to New York on December 21, 1963, when her 500 passengers spent Christmas at sea.
(Graphic Photos, Ltd.)

interior...

34

△ Just some of the delicious fresh fruit being prepared for Sylvania's passengers in March, 1960, by fruitman Edward Boyle (right) and his assistant, George Salmon. Edward's job entailed looking after all fresh fruit on board, from making up baskets of it to fruit cocktails served by the waiters.

◁ Sylvania's impressive tourist lounge incorporated columns of rare Canadian marble. (Cunard Archives)

▽ Sylvania . . . . . an example of the tourist class "A" deck four-berth cabins. (Cunard Archives)

interior...

△ *Bright, airy and spacious, Sylvania's tourist restaurant made a perfect setting for some memorable meals.* (Cunard Archives)

◁ *View from the stalls in Sylvania's cosy cinema, decorated in warm shades of red.* (Cunard Archives)

▽ *Tourist and first-class beauty parlour in the Sylvania.* (Cunard Archives)

interior...

Carinthia

Carinthia, sister Number 3 of the four 22,000-tonners built by the Cunard Steam-Ship Company for its Canadian service, had the distinction of being named by Royalty.

Princess Margaret launched her from John Brown's yard at Clydeside on December 14, 1955. The ceremony evoked many happy memories for the Princess, who said: "I remember so clearly my earlier visit here, when I watched my mother launch the ship which bears her name." That ship, of course, was the giant Queen Elizabeth, at 83,673 tons the biggest passenger liner in the world, launched by Queen Elizabeth (the Queen Mother) in September, 1938. (The Queen Mary, which celebrated her golden jubilee in 1986, was 80,774 tons). It was typically "royal weather" — bitterly cold, rain lashing down, with the crowds of shipyard and dockside workers and their families cheering from beneath a sea of umbrellas. Ignoring

A great liner in the making – Carinthia's superstructure being created amongst a maze of metal at Clydebank in April, 1956. But that big aluminium dome topping her funnel, now in place, denotes that she is nearing completion.
(Cunard Line)

her glass-plated shelter, Princess Margaret walked out into the rain to wave to them.

Captain Andrew MacKellar was appointed master of the new liner. He had commanded the Saxonia on her maiden voyage in 1954. London-born MacKellar had served as Staff Captain in both the "Queens", the Aquitania, Mauretania and Caronia. His first passenger liner command was the Ascania, from which he became master of the Media, Samaria, Scythia and Britannic. The Chief Engineer, Mr. Frank O. Summerfield, the Purser, Mr. John Stirling Dixon, and the Chief Steward, Mr. Owen J. Curtis, all came from Merseyside.

Although closely resembling her sisters, Saxonia and Ivernia, the Carinthia had interior decoration considerably different, with Tudor-Style smoking rooms, Regency-style first-class lounge and French rococo restaurant. Pompeii was the theme for the tourist restaurant. The beautiful chairs in the liner's first-class dining room, made from birchwood, with polished satin wood finished and inlaid with mahoghany, were originally made in 1913 for the old Aquitania. Another novel feature about Carinthia was the soda-fountain in her tourist section. Attendants Herbert Lawrenson, of Liverpool, and

Relatives, friends and bystanders wave farewell to the Carinthia as she swings out into mid-river, dressed overall, for her maiden voyage from Liverpool to New York in June, 1956. (D.P. & E.)

William Glavin, of Southport, spent three weeks in the United States learning the latest developments in soda-fountain technique. Among the ices, milk-shakes, sundaes, parfaits and fruit freezes, they were later able to serve the liner's passengers with the "Carinthia Special" — a banana split!

Carinthia left Liverpool on her maiden voyage on June 27, 1956. Crowds, with some spectators waving Union Jacks, gathered near

Prince's Landing Stage to bid her bon voyage. Many of her 870 passengers were emigrants, including 13 hard-rock metal miners, seeking a new life prospecting for gold, uranium and copper. Some of the male gathering doffed their hats and caps in farewell, but the magical moment of the ship's leaving, which will be remembered by most of those watching, happened when one of the young members of the crew dropped his cap. This fell on to a dumb barge as he was unshipping the last gangway. G.P.O. engineer Harry Daley, of Liverpool, retrieved the cap, but failed to throw it back to the ship. A rope from the liner solved the problem and the cap was duly hauled on board!

There was always something of interest going on in the Mersey – like Carinthia, pictured here inward bound from New York and preparing to tie up at the landing stage in March, 1959. (D.P. & E.)

Carinthia was the first of the four sisters ever to go cruising, when she made a Christmas and New Year cruise to the West Indies from New York in 1956.

In May, 1958, Carinthia made an extra-special call to Douglas Bay, Isle of Man. She had brought home 120 Manx ex-patriots from all parts of Northern America, who were visiting their lovely old island home. The Isle of Man Steam Packet Company's vessel, Manxman, acted as tender to bring them ashore.

Carinthia's surprise docking at Southampton, from Montreal, instead of at Liverpool in November, 1962, raised a few eyebrows. The Company explained that this was only a temporary measure for one trip because the Saxonia and the Ivernia had been taken out of service for exterior alterations and restyling for cruising, as I have already explained.

Carinthia and the Sylvania (which came into service on June 5, 1957), were among 15 liners, including the Queen Mary and the Queen Elizabeth, open to the public during the Ocean Travel Fortnight celebrations from November 4 — 16, 1963. Passes were obtained through 1,200 travel agents in Britain. Thousands of visitors to the ships had their very first taste of inspecting a luxury liner and found no difficulty in dreaming of how marvellous cruising in them could be!

In January, 1961, when Carinthia was dry-docked, ship-repair workers went on strike. She was left in the dry dock for 16 weeks, which caused doors to twist and stick. Joiners were hard pressed to get her serviceable again.

Then, in August, that year, in the foggy St. Lawrence, she was involved in a collision with the 7,000-ton Tadoussac, a Canadian vessel. Both ships suffered only slight damage.

Even in the heyday of commuting by ocean liner, not many people elected to travel across the North Atlantic during the stormy winter

Carinthia anchors in mid-stream, waiting for the Empress of Canada (left) to vacate her birth at Liverpool landing stage. (D.P.&E.)

Some of the Carinthia's catering staff leave the liner at Liverpool after a union meeting on July 7, 1960. An unofficial seamen's strike, in support of a pay and hours claim, eventually developed. Many ships nationwide were soon affected by the strike, but the Birkenhead-built Union Castle liner, Windsor Castle, at 38,000 tons the largest liner to be built in Britain for 21 years, managed to make her maiden voyage from Southampton to South Africa on August 18.

(D.P. & E.)

months and many of the regular service ships would become cruise ships in more moderate climes for the season. A striking example of this occurred in January, 1965. when the Carinthia arrived at Liverpool from New York and Halifax, Nova Scotia, with only eight first-class passengers, five of whom were members of one family. They had two stewards each to wait on them! Another passenger on the ship was a stowaway — a bird dubbed Beaky, which was found in the Carinthia's sundeck lounge. No one at the time could identify it — black and white and said to be rather like a penguin. It had been injured and some kind persons were ensuring that it would go to the RSPCA for treatment.

Post-war strikes in the ports were quite frequent, involving a number of unions and occurring for many reasons. These plagued the maritime trade and passenger liners frequently were affected by stoppages — often resulting from actions by their own crews. Whatever the rights involved in these disruptive disputes, ships sometimes missed consecutive sailing dates, and in retrospection, these obviously helped hasten the eventual end of regular long-distance passenger services. The seamen's strike of 1966, for instance, cost the Cunard Line £4,000,000.

Often, attempts were made to beat unofficial striking attempts and the great ships would put to sea without help from other than their own highly-skilled masters, officers and men. Sometimes, they even put to sea without a high proportion of their own striking crew

Teatime on board the Carinthia on August 17, 1960, but the liner was still in Huskisson Dock, Liverpool, her departure postponed when about half her crew failed to report for duty. Passengers later had to fly out to Canada.(D.P. & E.)

Delayed by a ship-repairers' strike for more than five months, the Carinthia finally leaves the Mersey for Canada on May 31, 1961.(Clayton Photos, Ltd.)

members. Like the Carinthia did, in March, 1965, when she left the Mersey with 200 passengers on board eleven hours behind schedule and with about 185 of her crew — mostly catering staff — missing from duty. She was due to call at Greenock en route for Quebec and Montreal, to pick up another 160 passengers, chiefly emigrants — and some crew replacements. They had walked out, on unofficial strike, over a new agreement on pay and hours. The Mersey ferryboat, Leasowe, was engaged as a tender to take the passengers and their luggage at Liverpool out to the liner, anchored in mid-river. The Greenock passengers, however, had been told that they could not sail in the undermanned liner and they left for Canada by other means — some by a charter flight and the others in the Queen Elizabeth from Southampton to New York. At least, the liner was able to take on extra crew at Greenock.

By 1966, Liverpool was seeing fewer and fewer passenger liners and where, at one time, the port was almost an automatic choice for the Liverpool-registered ships to be given their annual overhauls, orders had dwindled considerably. In September, 1966, hard on the heels of Cunard's announcement that the Sylvania was to be transferred from the Liverpool-New York service to Southampton, came news that only the Carinthia among the company's passenger ships was to be overhauled on Merseyside that winter. Southampton, it seemed was getting most of the cream. By October that year, the Carinthia was the only Cunard passenger liner on the Liverpool-Canada run.

Early in December, 1966, even Carinthia's 22,000-ton bulk could not cope with the great North Atlantic storm, which forced her to heave-to and made her 48 hours late on her homeward run from Canada. Conditions were so bad that she was ordered to omit her usual call at Greenock to disembark passengers. She had already lost time on her outward voyage when penned in dock at Liverpool for 48 hours in an earlier gale. On the eventual arrival of the liner at Liverpool with 290 passengers Captain Harry de Legh, her master, declared: "The barometer just kept going down and down. At 2 o'clock on Thursday morning, I would put the winds at hurricane force and we had to heave-to again for six hours."

That was Carinthia's last voyage of the year in the Canadian service and she went in for overhaul and refit for her fortnight's Christmas cruise out of Liverpool, on December 23, to the Atlantic Isles. Because of a damaged rudder, caused by the storm, it was touch and go whether the cruise would have to be cancelled. However, a double shift of men, working day and night for a week, saved disappointment for 550 passengers who had booked to spend Christmas in a summer climate. Even so, Carinthia had to forego her

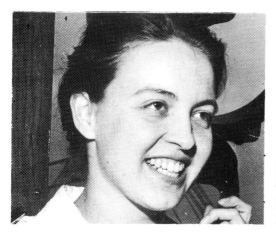

Valerie Nash, Carinthia's assistant purser, interpreted the vital medical instructions which helped to save a French sailor's life.

new cruise dress of white paint, as she sailed on schedule, with Captain Hugh Chaloner in command. Cruising continued to be the business mainstays to which the four sisters (and other Cunarders) clung for a long time.

In the April, following her cruise to the Atlantic Isles on February, 1967, Carinthia, back on her routine run between Liverpool and Canada, was homeward bound for Liverpool when she was involved in a vital mercy dash. She made a four-hour detour in answer to an urgent appeal from the French frigate, Cetra Columbia, seeking medical aid for an injured 34-year-old seaman, Yves Thepot, who had been badly crushed by falling machinery. Dr. James McKenzie Forbes, a general practitioner from Winchester, who was standing in for the liner's regular doctor, decided that the seaman required an operation and the Carinthia put into Cobh, Eire, where the sailor's leg was amputated.

It was round-the-clock care for him for four days and nights by Carinthia's medical team, which saved him. This included nursing sisters Margaret Wilson and Elizabeth Williams, who worked in 12-hour shifts to tend Yves. The patient was transferred from the freighter to the liner in one of the Cunarder's lifeboats — in the dark

Carinthia at Liverpool on April 6, 1967. Note her lion-with-world stem emblem. Her sister, Saxonia, was the first modern Cunarder to wear this. The emblem is placed in the "eyes" of the ship, where the figurehead used to be in a sailing ship. Of the four sisters, only Carinthia kept her original black hull to the end of her Cunard days. (D.P. & E.)

and in a full gale — in the charge of Chief Officer John Mortimer. Also in the lifeboat were Dr. Forbes and Mr. George Perry, the ship's dispenser. A most vital role in this drama was played by Miss Valerie Nash, the assistant purser. For an hour, while the lifeboat kept trying to get alongside the freighter in the heaving seas, Valerie translated a stream of instructions in French over the radio telephone between Captain Chaloner, on Carinthia's bridge, and the officers on the Cetra Columbia, who spoke no English.

Autumn that year saw the saga of the Cunard liners at Liverpool drawing to a close. With the sailing of the Carinthia from Liverpool to Montreal on October 13, the Cunard Steam-Ship Company's regular passenger services from the Mersey ceased. Cunard announced this grim news just 12 months after it had ended its Liverpool-New York service. Although this did not mean the complete disappearance of Cunarders from Liverpool's waterfront — a couple of cruises were planned for the Franconia out of Liverpool — it was virtually the end of a magnificent era.

As Carinthia slipped her mooring at Prince's Landing Stage, Liverpool, at 8.27 on that October night, and began to move slowly out of the Mersey, she gave a deep-throated salute on her siren. It was goodbye to her Liverpool home and she severed a link that had been forged 127 years earlier. Captain L.K. Goodier was her master at that time and with him were passengers who could hardly have been aware that they were taking part in one of the sad little scenes in maritime history. It took place, perhaps appropriately, on Friday 13.

Sylvania

The fourth of Cunard's "sparkling quartette", Sylvania completed the company's building programme for the Canadian passenger and cargo trade and was due to make her maiden voyage from Liverpool to Canada on June 5, 1957.

She was launched from John Brown's shipyard on November 22, the year before, by Mrs. Norman A. Robertson, wife of the Canadian High Commissioner in London. In general design, she was like her sisters and could accommodate nearly 900 passengers (154 first-class and 724 tourists), with a capacity for some 290,000 cubic feet of cargo, plus 12,000 cubic feet of insulated space. And, like her sisters, her domed funnel, massive bridge structure and curved, raked stem, contributed to her handsome appearance.

With two tugs on her bow and her decks crowded with passengers, Sylvania leaves Liverpool for a routine voyage to Quebec and Montreal.(Cunard Line)

The liner's first-class restaurant owed its decorative scheme to the famous Clifford's Inn Room at the South Kensington Museum, London. The use of finely-figured walnut contrasted with the intricate markings of white ash burr. The chairs were an adaptation of a very early 18th Century model in walnut. Her tourist restaurant, spanning the entire width of the hull, was decorated in white enamel with mouldings of gold aluminium. Murals, painted by Margot

Gilbert, depicted English fruit harvesting. The cinema, with stalls and balcony, on the promenade deck, was based on an old-fashioned music hall, with ample use of red hide quilting, red upholstery and red curtains imparting a cosy, warm atmosphere. Her first-class smokeroom and cocktail bar had a military decoration theme, based on badges of the British Army and their Canadian counterparts. Each badge was painted by Rana Stryck and they made a splendid frieze, particularly striking en masse over the bar and fireplace in all their heraldic colouring. As the smoking-room was primarily a place for men, it was thought that the badges would be a good topic for starting conversation!

The tourist-class smoking-room's decor was refreshingly original in that its 17 murals depicted proverbs of European countries, in their original language and with translations. These were executed by Denise Bates. The first-class lounge was modelled on the boudoir of Madame de Sérilly, with grey sycamore panels embellished with gold mouldings and mirrors, and ivory-lacquered furniture covered with delicate damask woven in material, which looked like silk but was man-made fibre. This room had an oval dance-floor, with bay windows port and starboard. Its 460 sq.ft. ceiling, of the same shape, was decorated with paintings, executed by Tom Luzny, depicting incidents in classical mythology. Sylvania's impressive tourist lounge, with spacious dance-floor and orchestra platform, boasted a rare Canadian marble specially obtained to reproduce its columns of scagliola. Flanked to port and starboard by the covered promenade deck, it was the largest public room in the ship. An interesting frieze was composed of monochrome paintings of metopes of the Parthenon, painted at the Liverpool College of Art.

Another voyage over, Sylvania prepares to tie up alongside the Isle of Man ferry, Tynwald, at Liverpool landing stage, in August, 1957.

I have given more detail to Sylvania's internal decor simply to give the reader some idea of the beauty, comfort and interest created in ships like these.

The Statue of Liberty hails Sylvania, dressed overall for her first visit to New York in December, 1957. (Cunard Line)

Because of the recent ship-repair strike about the time that Sylvania was due to sail on her maiden voyage from Liverpool, on June 5, she was compelled to sail from Greenock instead on that day. It will be remembered that Ivernia, too, sailed from the Clyde instead of Liverpool, in 1955, because of a similar dispute.

I was present at the Press luncheon on board Sylvania the day before she sailed on her maiden voyage. We were taken out to her by tender as she was anchored in the Clyde estuary. Mr. Frank Dawson, Cunard's general manager, referred to those trying times for the shipping fraternity, chiefly caused by labour troubles. "The last 15 months have probably been the most difficult of my 45 years' service with the company," he said. In spite of the setbacks, Mr. Dawson was optimistic about the future, even suggesting that "we may go on and build other Canadian ships . . . because we have a very great and abiding affection and regard for our Canadian cousins."

The Common Market then, so far as Britain was concerned, was still a long way off and Mr. Dawson declared that Canada was becoming more and more important in Britain's daily life. He said: "We have built these ships to assist in this traffic of passengers and goods between this country and Canada, which started four years ago with the Saxonia. He felt that the work which Cunard had done up to 1939 was preparing the seedbed and tilling the land for the harvest. There would be room for expansion with the increasing volume of traffic between the U.K. and Canada.

48

Mr. Dawson also praised the team spirit and co-operation which existed between Cunard and the shipbuilders, and he said that there was nothing in the world to approach such a wonderful partnership. "In the case of each of the four ships, we have had the temerity to advertise sailing dates 12 months before they actually happened," he said.

In the light of the great changes that were to take place in the not-so-far-distant future, those were brave words, I thought in retrospect, looking through some of my old notes.

Cunard's total share of the Canadian passenger trade, west and eastbound since 1947, to that date, totalled 614,000 people.

Sylvania certainly kept to her maiden voyage sailing date, thanks to John Brown and Company. Under her master, Captain Frederick G. Watts, she left Greenock for Canada on June 5 and Merseyside's first glimpse of her came at the end of her round voyage, when she reached Liverpool, dressed overall, at 1 p.m. on June 20. From Montreal she had maintained an average speed of 21.43 knots, the fastest eastbound crossing of the four sister ships on the Canadian service.

A very popular ship, Sylvania, like her sisters, was involved in the 1960 seamen's strike. But on August 10 that year, she managed to sail from Southampton to Montreal with a depleted crew and some of her passengers helping out with the catering. On the homeward trip it was a similar story. When volunteers were called for from among the passengers, the chief respondents were a party of 24 Girl Guides from all parts of Britain. They did their eight-hour stints a dozen at a time and from the pay they received they gave a donation to their headquarters. However, the liner's next scheduled sailing from Southampton had to be cancelled because of the continuing strike. But she lost only one round trip before the dispute was settled.

In November, 1960, as Sylvania arrived at Liverpool from Montreal, Cunard Line announced that she was to take the place of their famous 27,778-ton Britannic on the Liverpool-New York service. This was because Britannic was due to be put up for sale on her return to Liverpool on December 3 — the next month. So, in April, 1961, Sylvania (commanded by Captain A.E. Divers, master of the Britannic on her last voyage) operated with her two smaller sister ships, the neat little first-class 13,000-ton liners, Media and Parthia, on the Liverpool-New York run, calling regularly, both ways, at Cobh.

Having been prevented by gales from sailing from Liverpool to New York, via Greenock, in January, 1962, for 48 hours, Sylvania was hammered by another storm a few weeks later. On March 6, she arrived at Liverpool from New York, two days later. Her master, Captain J. Crosbie Dawson, said it was the worst passage that he had

Sylvania at Prince's Landing Stage, Liverpool on her arrival from Canada in August, 1960.
(D.P. & E.)

"Liverpool on her stern, bound to go," ran the old saying. Sylvania reveals her giant propellers during a winter overhaul in Canada Dock, Liverpool. Some of her 165 fathoms of anchor chain lie in the foreground.
(Clayton Photos Ltd.)

made for many years. "There was one period of about 12 hours when the winds were at 70 miles per hour," he said. Some of the liner's furniture was damaged and heaps of crockery smashed. The ship's doctor had to treat many of the passengers for sea-sickness and strained muscles — the latter caused by their lurching about as the ship rolled. Still, it's an ill wind that blows no good, as the saying goes, and a baby girl was born in the Sylvania on that rough passage. She was later named Sylvia Ann. Passengers and crew were thrilled by the babe's arrival and happily "wet her head".

That year saw Sylvania in a cruising mood, with four interspersed Atlantic sailing holidays from Liverpool to New York lined up. Prices started at £140 and included hotel accommodation and guided tours of New York's famous spots; a visit to the seaside resort of Atlantic City and the Circle Line cruise around Manhattan Island. The two Queens also were doing their stint on a bigger scale and bringing America within reach of holidaymakers who could afford to stay in Manhattan for eight days.

During the national Ocean Travel Fortnight, more than 1,500 people applied for permission to visit the Sylvania when she was "at home" to the public at Liverpool's Huskisson Dock for three days in November, 1962 — the sixth anniversary of her launching. Many other famous liners also were on view at the various British ports on those special annual occasions.

Unlike the bird which was to drop in on her sister, Carinthia, in the following January, the feathered visitor that fell exhausted on to Sylvania's deck in May, 1964, was identified by experts. Captain Hugh Chaloner, a member of Britain's Northern Zoological Society, recognised the bird as being rare in Europe and arranged for it to be taken to Chester Zoo, near to Liverpool. After the next voyage, Captain Chaloner was informed that his little stowaway was a yellow-crested flicker and a native of America's eastern coast.

The brotherhood of the sea is such that even the great ocean liners will deviate hundreds of miles from their courses to aid stricken ships and sailors in distress. Sylvania made some errands of mercy, too. In June, 1964, when in the North Atlantic and bound for Liverpool from New York, Captain Chaloner received an urgent radio message for medical assistance just before midnight. He ordered a 90-degree turn to the south and Sylvania made full speed for 12 hours to meet the American Coast Guard weather ship, Coos Bay, on Station Echo, midway between Bermuda and the Azores.

An emergency operation for appendicitis was performed on chief gunner's mate Fred Diefenbacher, of New York, by the liner's surgeon, Dr. R.C. Hartley, assisted by Dr. N.C. Reid, a senior medical registrar at Liverpool's Broadgreen Hospital. Dr. Reid was returning to Britain with his wife and family after working in the United States for a year. Fred, who was able to walk off the Sylvania

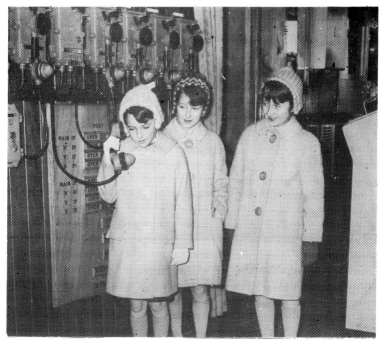

Three little maids from school . . . Sisters Gladys, Susan and Sylvia McRea pictured having fun in the Sylvania at Liverpool in November, 1962, when the liner was open to the public. (D.P. & E.)

at Liverpool on his way to an American hospital in Manchester, thanked the medical team and added: "I guess I am a lucky man. Everybody on board the Sylvania was terrific." And from the commanding officer of the Coos Bay came this radio message: "The United States Coast Guard thoroughly appreciates your help and realises what this entailed. Once again, the brotherhood of the sea has saved a sailor's life. Bon voyage and God speed."

Nearly a year later, Sylvania, this time outward bound from Liverpool to New York, and in charge of Captain Chaloner, again changed course to hurry to the aid of the Norwegian freighter, Lionne, about 740 miles south of Greenland. Twenty-five of the freighter's 27 crew were rescued after abandoning their sinking ship in heavy seas. Sylvania picked up 12 men from a lifeboat and another Norwegian freighter, the Raila, rescued the remainder. The two men who perished were swept away by huge waves when their liferaft capsized.

Sick crew member Fred Diefenbacher, from the weather ship Coos Bay (right), is taken on board the Sylvania for emergency medical treatment which saved his life. (John Partington)

The Cunarder Sylvania arriving in the Mersey in February, 1965, after her extensive overhaul. She left soon afterwards on Cunard's first cruise out of Liverpool since 1939. Part of New Brighton old pier can be seen on the right. (Bob Bird, Wallasey)

In May, 1964, Syvania collected passengers from Boston. This was the first time that a Cunarder had visited that port since 1949. The call proved an economic success, as a result of which the liner was scheduled to call at Boston on five occasions the following year.

After an overhaul and some extensive improvements to her passenger accommodation — back at her birthplace in John Brown's yard — Sylvania returned to the Mersey on February 6, 1965, to operate the first Cunard cruise from Liverpool since an earlier Sylvania, in 1939 — the year that the last war began. More than 100

Two pretty ladies . . . . . Jill Ridgeway, of Birkenhead (then 18), enjoys a warm September day and a close-up view of sunlit Sylvania, at anchor, from the deck of a Mersey ferry boat. (D.P. & E.)

staterooms on 'A' deck were completely reconditioned and equipped with private showers and toilets. A temporary outdoor swimming pool was constructed and new soft-furnishing schemes were provided in the tourist-class public rooms.

Dressed overall and with bands playing some jolly music, she sailed, with Captain H.E. Stonehouse, carrying 500 passengers on a 27-day Mediterranean holiday cruise, taking in eight ports. Costs ranged from £190 to £530. Sylvania left in blustery weather, under grey skies and returned from the cruise in fog . . . small wonder that Merseysiders were seeking the sun!

This venture created quite a stir on Merseyside because nearly all the money-making passenger traffic was based at Southampton.

Canadian Pacific had already operated a few cruises from Liverpool, but as cruising then was becoming increasingly popular and so many other big shipping concerns also were involved, the "jam" was spreading more thinly all the time .

After another long seamen's strike in 1966, the Sylvania actually sailed without passengers on a rushed voyage from Liverpool to Canada to pick up passengers waiting at Quebec and Montreal. Having landed these passengers at Southampton, in July, she picked up stores and fuel and again sailed "empty" to Merseyside to carry out her normal scheduled sailing from Liverpool to New York. The liner made something of a record in that this probably was the fastest-ever turnround of a Cunard liner in Liverpool. A company spokesman said: "This is the first time that an empty liner will have arrived and departed with nearly 500 passengers, within three hours." Sylvania generally operated on the Liverpool-New York run in those days, but she had to make her fast voyage in ballast because of the problems of getting the Queen liners and the Carmania and the Franconia back into service quickly from Southampton.

When Sylvania left Liverpool for New York on November 24, 1966, the express passenger link between the two cities, which had existed for more than a century, was broken. The weekly cargo service, however, was continued. Cunard announced that the passenger service was being closed so that Sylvania could be transferred to the company's Southampton-Quebec-Montreal run. This freed the Franconia to operate a luxury cruise service from New York to Bermuda, which Cunard took over at the invitation of the Bermudan Government as a valuable, dollar-earning operation.

One of the saddest members of Sylvania's crew was 75-year-old refrigerator greaser, John Dacey, who had sailed out of Liverpool since 1910. Cunard's decision to switch the liner to Southampton had quite upset him. Said John: "I am an old man now, and the ship is my real home . . . I know that if I leave the sea, I couldn't live for very long on land . . . ." Some 400 Merseysiders manned the Sylvania.

The liner featured in a hovercraft experiment at Southampton in January, 1967, when a trial on-and-off loading of an SRN-6 hovercraft was conducted on board. The idea was to study the feasibility of loading and unloading the craft which, if successful, could result in passengers being able to go sightseeing at cruise ports in the liner's own hovercraft. It was agreed that this sort of operation also would help boost Britain's invention round the world.

Cunard launched its new fly-cruise holidays with the now white-painted Sylvania in February, 1967. Passengers flew out to Gibraltar, cruised around the Atlantic Isles in the liner then flew home from "The Rock". The liner's hovercraft was used for joy-rides and sightseeing trips on that cruise.

I often used to sit in some of the grand public rooms of the Liverpool liners, perhaps waiting for, or having interviewed, some of the passengers. And I generally thought how I, too, would like to be waiting for my afternoon tea or dinner to be served in such luxurious surroundings on those sailing days, with all the delightful prospects of the voyage ahead. But the repeated vocal warnings over a ship's loudspeaker system of "All visitors ashore; all visitors ashore, please!" plus the odd blast on the ship's siren, quickly shattered one's dreams. These occasions also often engendered sad scenes. Sad, certainly for those visitors who came on board with their special company passes to say farewell to loved ones — generally emigrating and, sometimes, as with the elderly, in the knowledge that they might not see one another again.

There have been times, of course, when, perhaps carried away by the joyful or tearful emotion of departure, that the "visitors ashore" warnings have gone unheard or unheeded . . . like the time three men and a girl failed to hear this nautical "Time, please!" while chatting in the Sylvania at Southampton in February, 1967. Sylvania had cast off her bow and stern ropes and was well on the move when the red-faced quartette found that they were bound for a grand cruise to the sunny Atlantic Isles!

They were Mr. Chris Ponsford, a company director, of Southampton, his brother, Anthony, of Winchester, a sales manager, Miss Jackie Hunt, and her boyfriend, John Walter, of Sparsholt, near Winchester. The brothers had gone on board to see their parents off on the cruise and the other couple were with them. Because the sea was too rough for the Isle of Wight pilot boat to put them ashore, they had to stay with the liner from Southampton to Madeira . . . but I bet they wished that they had had time to pack!

In August that year, Cunard confirmed the success of the company's fly-cruise programme with British European Airways in the Mediterranean and promised a considerably extended similar programme the next year, using Naples as the new base port. In addition, the company announced that the United States-based cruises to the Caribbean would also be opened to the U.K. holidaymakers in special fly-out-sail-back (or vice versa) package holidays, in arrangement with British Overseas Airways Corporation.

But only two months later came the bombshell . . . . The Cunard Steam-ship Company was to cut their shore staff by 65 per cent and withdraw three more passenger ships from service. Sir Basil Smallpeice, Cunard's chairman, who announced this unexpected fiscal surgery in London on October 19, 1967, said that the company had made a pre-tax loss of £2,031,000 in the first half of the current year, with the passenger side of the business losing more than that figure. The all-year-round cruise liner, Caronia, and the Carinthia,

Farewell, Sylvania! Mersey shipping sounded their sirens in salute as the Cunarder left Liverpool for her last scheduled voyage from the port on November 24, 1966. This marked the end of the regular passenger service which existed between Liverpool and New York for 120 years.(Bob Bird, Wallasey)

were pulled out of service before Christmas, with the Sylvania to follow in the May after completing her advertised fly-cruise. The liners would be put up for sale and some 1,000 permanent employees among the 1,450 crew members would become redundant. The remainder were short-service staff. This shock statement followed the sale of the Queen Mary and the pending sale of the Queen Elizabeth.

Sir Basil blamed the 1966 seamen's strike, which had cost the company about £4 million and left it too weak to keep Caronia, Carinthia and Sylvania running. In a message to the staff, the chairman said: "This is a sad day. But for those who look to a future in our reduced three-ship passenger fleet — and we want to retain as many as possible of the best-qualified of our regular Cunard officers, ratings and shore staff — it is the basis of a new and realistic phase in Cunard history." This company streamlining was taken even further at the end of January, 1968, when a major reorganisation of the board of directors resulted in their number being reduced from thirteen to nine.

Sylvania, for her short allotted span with Cunard, carried on. She sailed from New York on December 11, 1967, with 462 passengers and picked up 77 more at Halifax, Nova Scotia, as the only Cunard liner making a North Atlantic Christmas voyage. Five years earlier, five Cunarders including the Queens, had made the North Atlantic Christmas crossing, carrying more than 4,000 passengers.

On January 31, 1968, it was confirmed that Carinthia and Sylvania had been bought by the Sitmar Line, of Genoa, at prices thought to be £1 million each. They were eventually renamed Fairland and Fairwind, respectively, and replaced the 12,478-ton Castel Felice and the 13,317-ton Fairsea, on the Australian service. A condition of sale prevented the two ships from competing on any of Cunard's regular routes and they were also precluded from leaving British ports on cruises. Fairland (later to be renamed Fairsea) and Fairwind were converted in Italy, each to carry about 1,000 one-class passengers — at a total cost of nearly £15 million, to sail on the England-Australia run. Fairwind later was based at Fort Lauderdale, Florida, operating cruises to the Caribbean, Mexico and Puerto Rico.

Footnote:
The former Cunard quads are still in service at the time of writing this (May, 1988), cruising in various parts of the world.

Carmania and Franconia, under the Russian flag, have not changed externally from their Cunard days and retain their distinctive dome-top funnels.

Carinthia and Sylvania are still serving the Sitmar Line and cruise from east and west coast ports of America. Both have been extensively altered, with new-shape funnels and superstructure and bear little resemblance to their Russian sister-ships.

Empress of Scotland (I) & (II)

When the tall, three-funnelled Empress of Scotland (II) glided up the Mersey early on a summer morning, sparkling white against a blue-sky backdrop and the green of the Wirral bank, home again after another long voyage to Canada, she made a living picture-postcard. Many people thought that she was the loveliest ship to grace the Mersey, with her slightly raked stem and cruiser stern.

She had lofty, stately rooms, one of which included a musicians' gallery, and her general regal style belonged to a design of between-wars luxury liners, which all too soon were to be replaced by modern silhouettes and small-room interiors. This 26,313-ton Canadian Pacific flagship was very much a long-lived daughter of proud Mother Liverpool, although she spent more than a quarter of her life in the Pacific under another name.

Built and engined by the Fairfield Shipbuilding and Engineering Company, she was launched in fog at Glasgow on December 17, 1929, as Empress of Japan, for CPR's Pacific service between Vancouver and Japan and China. Holiday crowds watched her arrive in the Mersey from the Clyde in June, 1930, and admired her artistic colour schemes. Unlike most of the Canadian Pacific liners, she had three funnels, painted buff, with white hull and a blue band along the line of the maindeck, giving her the appearance of a huge yacht. And thousands turned out to give the new ship the once-over at her berth in Gladstone Dock, Bootle. For a shilling a time, they saw how the wealthy were going to travel with her in grand style, and marvelled that her passenger facilities also included a "talkie" cinema.

The Empress of Japan made a name for herself immediately by making a record-breaking maiden voyage from Liverpool to Quebec a few days later, on June 14. She returned to Southampton and then left for Hong Kong, and her new station at Vancouver. She made her first Pacific voyage from Yokohama to Victoria, British Colombia, cutting 4 hours 20 minutes from the previous best time. And this lovely Pacific queen, with a given speed of 23 knots (plus a wide reserve margin for a good timekeeping!) held that ocean's "blue riband" throughout her long reign there.

She became the largest and the fastest ship on the Pacific Ocean, holding all speed records until the outbreak of the second world war when, two months later, in November, 1939, she was requisitioned and converted into a troopship. Her duties took her to theatres of war all over the world.

Still sailing as Empress of Japan, in 1940 she sustained slight machinery damage from a near-miss bomb in the North Atlantic. No

*Empress of Scotland (II), launched in 1929 as the Empress of Japan, was one of
the loveliest ships to grace the Mersey. Here she is sailing in the St. Lawrence as
the Empress of Japan.* (Associated Press)

*This fine model of Canadian Pacific's first Empress of Japan (5,905 tons) was
discovered in 1968 in a Rotterdam cellar . . . hidden away before the invasion of
Holland in 1940. An elegant, yacht-like liner, she sailed from Liverpool on her
maiden voyage to Vancouver in April, 1891. She left Canadian Pacific's
ownership in 1925 and changed hands twice to be broken up at Vancouver in
1926.* (Tom Kroeze, Rotterdam)

less than her master, Captain J.W. Thomas, of Vancouver, and her Chinese quartermaster, Ho Kan, in an incredible "dynamic-duo" partnership, saved the great white Empress from virtual destruction on this occasion. Captain Thomas had given evasive-action orders to the quartermaster as the latter swung the wheel while lying on his stomach to avoid machine-gun bullets raking the bridge! Both men were later decorated for their bravery. Two bombs struck the liner but glanced off her into the sea to cause no vital damage.

The liner's luck held out again when she was bombed in the Sundra Straits on her way to Singapore, on leaving with 1,200 of the last women and children from the island on passage to Batavia.

Appropriately, Captain Thomas was the focal point of another amazing incident, in May, 1948, when (as Empress of Scotland) the liner was sailing to Liverpool with 1,700 Middle East service personnel on what was to have been her last troop-carrying assignment before returning to peacetime duties. A dove alighted on her bridge, ten miles before the Mersey Bar Lightship. The bird then settled on Captain Thomas' shoulder and stayed there until the Empress tied up at Liverpool Landing Stage! Captain Thomas retired soon after that voyage.

Japan's entry into the war created embarrassment about the liner's name and, on October 16, 1942, she was renamed Empress of Scotland to become the company's second ship to bear that name.

* * *

To digress a little . . . CPR'S first Empress of Scotland was the former German liner, the 25,000-ton Kaiserin Auguste Victoria, built at Stettin in 1906 for the Hamburg-Amerika Line and surrendered to Britain in 1919 under the Versailles Treaty. For some months, she worked for the Americans, carrying troops home from Europe, and in February 14, 1920, she made her first voyage from Liverpool to New York under charter to Cunard. In May, 1921, she was bought by C.P. from the Reparations Commission and on August 5 was renamed Empress of Scotland and converted into an oil-burner.

Her first voyage for Canadian Pacific was on January 22, 1922, from Southampton to New York, followed by a chartered cruise to the Mediterranean. In June, 1923, she was in collision with the steamer Bonus at Hamburg, and in January, the next year, she left New York on the company's first Mediterranean cruise. During the years that she was the pride of the company, she was the largest liner entering Canada and she carried the Prince of Wales and Prince George in September, 1927, on their return from touring that country.

C.P.R.'s first Empress of Scotland, the former German liner, Kaiserin Auguste Victoria. Among the works of art on board were pictures painted by the Kaiserin herself. (Canadian Pacific)

Following the Titanic's sinking, she had been fitted with a powerful searchlight, which could illuminate an object five miles away. She was also the liner which carried the first talking picture equipment ever installed in a Canadian ship.

On completion of her 71st Atlantic voyage, in October, 1930, Empress of Scotland was laid up at Southend and was then sold in December for scrap to a Blyth shipbreaker for £60,000. She was on show at Blyth for a time, when the public was given the opportunity of seeing her magnificent furnishings and fittings — some of her art items were oils painted by the Kaiserin.

Before these could be removed, however, and while the Empress was being prepared for a charity dance in her Mayfair ballroom, fire broke out on December 10 and spread too quickly to be controlled, although 18 holes were cut in her side. She sank at her berth and broke in two when being moved on June 1 the next year, and was finally demolished in October.

* * *

To return to the last Empress of Scotland. . . . Mr. Tom R. Patten, who joined the Empress before she left the builder's yard at Govan, served in her for many years, first as chief baker and then as chief confectioner. He told me that from the time the first troops boarded the Empress of Scotland at Melbourne on January 11, 1940, until February 10, 1945, some 5,881,762 meals were served on board.

"This lucky ship travelled 271,546 miles unescorted during the war," said Mr.Patten, who was among the few on the skeleton staff which took the liner, as Empress of Japan, to Hong Kong, where many Chinese signed on as crew. "Captain Thomas told me on VJ-Day that he and I were the only two men who had sailed in her from the beginning of hostilities."

In the light of today's "women's lib" and general shoulder-shrugging to any mention of sex, it seems almost ridiculous now that only just after the last war, women sunbathing on the decks of a troop-carrying liner caused quite a stir. The liner was the Empress of Scotland, returning to Liverpool from India in July, 1946, with 2,000 servicemen and 400 civilian passengers.

She had set out in monsoon heat and some of the girls quickly changed into their swimsuits, beachsuits and shorts. But because one or two elderly passengers complained, and the troops whistled and cheered (as troops always will) when the girls strolled by, the officer in charge had the delicate task of lecturing some of the ladies who, it was thought, had been a little "indiscreet in their dress".

Today, we have ships which virtually sail themselves because their equipment is so sophisticated. And, while a dwindling company of rugged "Cape Horners", who served under sail, still survive to swap yarns in their retirement, for some years many masters, smothered in paperwork and accountancy, have frankly regarded their vocations more as ships' managers-cum-wages-clerks. Such is the price of

The Empress of Japan was renamed Empress of Scotland (II) in 1942. Here she is sailing in the St. Lawrence, wearing the new house-flag insignia on her funnels. (Canadia Pacific)

progress, and while one can only laud the moves in invention and design, which leave so little to chance, modernisation must also have absorbed much of the sailor's initiative and creative abilities.

A good example of the old-time seaman who could be relied on to turn his hand to almost anything in an emergency, was the Empress of Scotland's carpenter, Mr. Gordon Vaggers. In 1947, Gordon worked like a demon to build a timber "iron-lung" in an attempt to save the life of a young airman on board, stricken with poliomyelitis. Gordon's efforts were in vain. The man died before the sailor could finish the job. But the "lung" remained on board as part of the liner's surgical equipment.

During six years of war, and the aftermath service as a trooper, Empress of Scotland steamed 608,000 miles and carried 258,000 troops, prisoners of war, civilians, "Python"-leave servicemen, American and Canadian brides and babies. Small wonder that after her return to Liverpool on May 3, 1948, on her last trooping voyage, that a two-year conversion in the hands of her original builders was called for.

Like a great white butterfly after metamorphosis, she emerged in May, 1950, as a luxury liner again. Her hull was painted white, with green boot topping and a green band, and on each side of her buff funnels was reproduced Canadian Pacific's red-and-white chequered house-flag design. Her broad promenade deck was now enclosed for its entire length. She was ready to sail on regular voyages from Liverpool to Canada with the Empress of Canada and the Empress of France.

As the company's new flagship, with improved accommodation for a total of 663 passengers, 452 fewer than her pre-war capacity, she left Liverpool on this first post-war commercial voyage on May 9, and in wintertime she earned more dollars by cruising out of New York. In April, 1952, her tall masts were shortened by 40 feet. This

An historic picture . . . Empress of Scotland, carrying Princess Elizabeth and Prince Philip, rounding the north coast of Ireland about 2 p.m. on Friday, November 16, 1951, north east of Inishtrahull Sound. One of the escorting destroyers can be seen faintly to the right of the liner's bow. The picture was transmitted by radio to the Liverpool Echo from a De Havilland Rapide aircraft. (D.P. & E.)

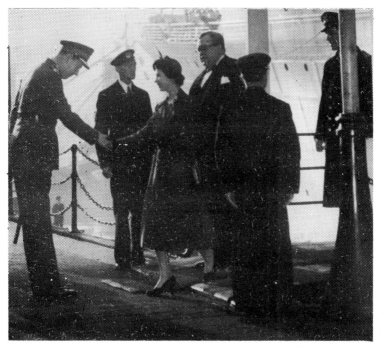

Lord Derby, as Lord Lieutenant of Lancashire, welcomes Princess Elizabeth and Prince Philip home, as the Royal couple step ashore from the Empress of Scotland at Liverpool on November 17, 1951. (D.P. & E.)

enabled her to pass under the Quebec Bridge and up the St. Lawrence to Montreal, which became her Canadian terminal port. She was then the largest liner in the world to reach Montreal.

It was the Empress of Scotland which brought the then Princess Elizabeth and Prince Philip to Liverpool in November, 1951, after their tour of Canada and visit to the United States. The Canadian destroyers, Micmac and Ontario, were the liner's escorts on her departure, and the Royal Navy destroyers, Creole and Zambesi, met her off Ireland to escort her to the Mersey. Beflagged Liverpool gave the royal couple a rousing welcome with gun salutes and trumpet fanfares as they arrived, still with their "Mountie" escort, to visit the Town Hall and the Anglican Cathedral.

Before they left the ship, the senior bellboy, George Newcombe, from Bebington, handed the Princess two dolls — a peasant girl and a comic sailor — for young Princess Anne and Prince Charles.

Princess Elizabeth had travelled for the first time in a large liner and she was lavish in her praise for the Empress of Scotland, even though the Empress had treated her with less than royal dignity, having rolled nearly all the way home in rough seas.

This voyage was a highlight in the long and distinguished career of Captain Cecil E. Duggan (an Old Conway, he "crossed the bar" in November, 1978). And during that royal voyage he received this signal: "Conways dining in London with the Earl Mountbatten of Burma as guest, have confidence that you will safeguard his Niece and Nephew in the crossing of the Ocean."

The Empress of Scotland's company praised the Princess. As Mrs. Ruth Hunt, of Liverpool, a member of the liner's hairdressing staff, put it: "The Princess makes everyone feel so much at ease during a conversation that she becomes everyone's sweetheart."

The couple orginally were to have returned home in the Empress of France — an arrangement upset by the King's illness — and the furnishings intended for the France were altered and transferred to the Scotland. A quick redecoration was given to the royal apartments, which included separate cabins and a combined dining and sitting-room for the Princess and the Duke. The whole section was partitioned off to ensure privacy.

Empress of Scotland tied up at Prince's Landing Stage, for the last time, on November 26, 1957, after her 187th crossing of the Atlantic between Liverpool and Montreal since refitting in 1950. She is framed in part by the overhanging flight-deck of H.M.S. Ocean. A farewell party was held "but everyone seemed to be too sad to make merry", said a crew member. (D.P. & E.)

This homeward voyage opened up a new phase in the pioneer achievements of the Liverpool Daily Post and Echo, two of whose photographers, Oswald (Ossie) Valentine and Peter Ralph, in a twin-engined Rapide aircraft, flew out to sea to a point off Inishtrahull, Northern Ireland, and photographed the liner making full speed for Liverpool among the "white horses". They developed the plates in an improvised darkroom in the plane, and the prints were transmitted by radio to the Echo Offices in time for the evening newspaper.

During the voyage, the unassuming Princess walked unannounced into the tourists' film show, took a back seat and refused better accommodation when stewards recognised her. "First come, first served," said the practical Princess.

* * *

The cold winds of recession increased in the 'Fifties, and by autumn, 1957, the fate of the Empress of Scotland hung in the balance. She was taken off the next year's sailing list. On September 23, Canadian Pacific announced that she was for sale. Her place on the Liverpool-Greenock-Montreal service was to be taken by the new flagship, Empress of Britain, launched by the Queen at Fairfield's yard in 1955.

In a chill wintry mist, on November 26, 1957, with Captain S.W. Keay in command, she tied up at Prince's Landing Stage, Liverpool, for the last time as Canadian Pacific's liner. Aged 28, she was ready for sale. Captain Keay, master of the Empress of Scotland for the previous 20 months, breakfasted alone on board that morning. "This is the real end of her passenger-liner life and everybody is feeling the parting very much," he said. "The Empress of Scotland is a grand old lady of the sea. She has done wonderful service and everyone who has served in her must be proud of her," he added.

Sentiments like these were not uncommon among masters leaving their old commands, and the crews who have served in these fine ships. They simply prove just how much a good ship can "grow" on those who sail in her.

Although the old girl was leaving the Mersey forever — appropriately she left on the last day of the year — she was at least heading for a £1 million facelift and a new lease of life in the skilled hands of the Hamburg-Atlantik Shipping Company, who converted her into the two-funnelled Hanseatic for the Hamburg-New York run. Still an "Empress" under the skin, and a great liner to the end, like her predecessor she was finally damaged by fire. This happened in New York in September, 1966. Towed back to Hamburg for scrap in December that year, she died in the same month of her birth.

Empress of Ireland

It may seem strange that a disaster, which took place more than 3,000 miles away, turned Liverpool into a city of mourning. But that happened when the Empress of Ireland sank in May, 1914.

Although wider-ranging tragedies and shocks were to be experienced soon afterwards in the Great War, which broke out in August that year, this loss of 1,024 souls — 90 per cent of the crew from Merseyside — was almost like the Titanic trauma all over again.

Empress of Ireland and her virtual twin, Empress of Britain the first (later renamed Montroyal and scrapped in 1930), both built at Fairfield's yard in Govan as twin-screw steamers over 14,000 tons and with speeds over 20 knots, were the largest and fastest ships in the Canadian trade in 1906. Both made their maiden voyages from Liverpool to Quebec that year; Empress of Britain on May 5 and Empress of Ireland on June 29. And they soon captured the East-West records from their nearest rivals, the Victorian and the Virginian of the Allan Line, later to be taken over by Canadian Pacific. For three years, each sailed almost every alternate fortnight, and when the Empress of Ireland left Quebec for Liverpool on the fine, clear night of May 28, 1914, with 1,057 passengers, Captain Henry Kendall and his crew of 420 were expecting just another routine voyage.

She dropped her pilot near Father Point, steamed down the St. Lawrence River and set course for the Gulf and the open ocean at a speed of between 17 and 18 knots. Meanwhile, only a few miles away, the 3,561-ton Norwegian collier, Storstad, was making her way inwards from Nova Scotia through the Gulf to Quebec. She was carrying 11,000 tons of coal . . . .

On the bridge of the Empress stood Captain Kendall who, some years earlier, had served as chief officer in the same ship. Born in Chelsea, he had spent most of his boyhood in Liverpool. He was a former cadet in the tough Mersey training ship, Indefatigable, from which he once ran away, was recaptured and brutally flogged. Henry served his apprenticeship in sail and once served in the Liverpool, the world's largest sailing ship. He had an extraordinary career and as a young apprentice was witness to a murder on a sailing ship in Australia. When his brother apprentice died in suspicious circumstances, Henry "got the message" and deserted to the goldfields to save his own life. He later joined the pearl fishers at Torres Strait and, although not yet 20, made a great reputation for himself among the islanders there. They called him "Maraki Maraki," or "the devil that knows all things." In April, 1908, he obtained his first C.P. command — the Milwaukee.

A highly-qualified seaman, Captain Kendall was already very well known as the former master of the C.P.R. liner, Montrose, who had recognised among his passengers the notorious British murderer, Dr. Hawley Crippen. And it was Kendall who sent the wireless message which resulted in Crippen's arrest on the ship's arrival in Canada from Liverpool in July, 1910. Crippen was travelling as Mr. John Robinson, with his mistress, Ethel Le Neve, disguised as "master" Robinson, his son. Kendall had grown curious about the pair ever since the ship had left Liverpool and he had studied newspaper pictures of the wanted Crippen. Blanking out the moustache, he immediately recognised the picture as that of "Mr. Robinson".

Crippen was said to have gold fillings in his teeth, and by inviting the pair to dine with him, Kendall managed to get Mr. Robinson to laugh heartily. That was the last time the mild little doctor saw anything funny in life again. Kendall had spotted the gold fillings as Crippen opened his mouth.

Satisfied that he had the murderer on board, Kendall informed Scotland Yard by wireless and after a series of messages over the air, Detective Chief Inspector Walter Dew took the faster White Star liner, Laurentic, to Canada and was waiting for the "Robinsons" when they arrived in the St. Lawrence in the Montrose on July 30. Arrested early next morning and escorted back to England, Crippen was put on trial and eventually hanged. Ethel Le Neve faded from the scene . . . .

Coincidentally, it was the famous Liverpool character and pub owner, "Ma" Egerton, who first started the police search for Crippen and his mistress. Ma was in a London pub one night when she spotted Ethel Le Neve wearing jewellery, which she recognised as that belonging to Belle Elmore, Dr. Crippen's wife, whom she knew and who had been reported missing for some time. Her information to the police led to the search of Crippen's house, the finding of Belle's body, and the big hunt for Crippen and Le Neve.

Captain Kendall was learning photography at the time Crippen was on board his ship. Thinking that the police might need a photograph of the suspect, he used the only plate he had for the picture, taken just before the liner reached Father Point. He hurriedly developed the plate but unfortunately placed this by a lamp to dry — and the film melted!

* * *

When Captain Kendall saw Storstad's lights about two miles away, he calculated that the two ships would pass starboard to starboard on parallel courses, with more than adequate space between them. And then came the unexpected. A thick blanket of fog glided across the St. Lawrence and within minutes there was a collision.

Storstad's bow cut deeply into the Empress between her two funnels. The collier's jammed anchor acted like a great can-opener to batter plates and lacerate some of the liner's human contents.

The tragic details told at the inevitable inquiry made depressing reading in the world's press. It was Lord Mersey who presided — the same president who conducted the Titanic enquiry only two years earlier. He was also to conduct the inquiry into the sinking of the Falaba, torpedoed in St. George's Channel on March 28, 1915, with the loss of more than 100 passengers and crew, followed by the Lusitania, torpedoed on May 7, the same year, in which 1,300 died. Liverpool-born Viscount Mersey of Toxteth, as he was known, was formerly Mr. Justice Bingham. He had a brilliant legal brain and at one time was M.P. for Liverpool's Exchange Division. He died, aged 89, at Littlehampton, on September 3, 1929, exactly a decade to the day before the outbreak of the second world war, which was to write another morbid list of sunken ships, with a horrific toll of life.

Captain Kendall told how, immediately after the collision, he shouted to Storstad's master, Captain Thomas Andersen, to keep his engines on full-ahead so that his vessel would continue to plug the ragged hole she had made. But Storstad had gone astern and the sea poured into the stricken liner.

Yet Captain Andersen's evidence was often in direct conflict with that of Captain Kendall. He denied emphatically that his vessel had backed off after the collision. He had ordered his engines ahead, he said, but the Empress of Ireland had moved away and bent the collier's bow over to port. He strongly denied that he had steamed a mile away, as suggested, and declared that he kept Storstad as close to the scene as possible.

The disaster occurred at 1.30 a.m., when most of the liner's passengers were asleep and certainly below. Because of this, naturally, many were slow in leaving their cabins and were very bewildered in the ensuing nightmare of blowing whistles and sirens. Some poured out on to the open decks within a few minutes, but the great liner, which had spelled comfort, warmth and security for them, could not wait for all. She sank within 14 minutes. With something like 60,000 gallons of seawater a second bursting through the 25ft. × 14ft. hole in her side, she rapidly began to heel over to starboard.

Hundreds of those still above the cataracts of water below were confronted with crazily-angled staircases, passages and companion.-ways, which nothing but a fly could scale. Men, women and children simply drowned in the darkness like mice in a water-butt with the lid

Some of the finest ships in the world were among the 100, which stretched down river for ten miles on the occasion of the King's inspection in July, 1913. In this section, before Liverpool Landing Stage, are, left to right: Mauretania, Media, Empress of Ireland and Orissa. Carmania and Ceramic were there, too. This was the year before the Great War and only ten months before the Empress of Ireland was sunk. (Canadian Pacific)

on. Many of the 700 who made the open decks fared little better as the Empress collapsed on her side and made her steaming, bubbling, dying plunge below the cold water.

Hundreds had been clinging to her port rails, shrieking and praying for the help that no one could give at that time in the fog and the cold and the dark. Some boats were lowered and one was crushed as the liner rolled on top of it. Victims were battered by heavy equipment sliding down the steeply-sloping decks, or entangled in the ropes and bric-a-brac. Others were sucked down in the great whirlpool as the liner sank, bodies bumping into bodies, desperate fingers of the non-swimmers groping for those floating or swimming.

Thanks to the courage of Empress of Ireland's two wireless-operators, Ferguson and his junior, Bamford (later commended at the court of inquiry), an S.O.S. was speedily tapped out and rescue operations began. In addition to the Storstad, which launched her boats and took on board some 75 survivors, (including Captain Kendall, who insisted on continuing the search for more), the pilot-vessel, Eureka (well-named, it seems), found the site in the fog, together with the tender, Lady Evelyn. They collected some 400 survivors, many of whom had simply kept swimming, with others who had clung to pieces of wood and the general flotsam, which

71

sinking ships shrug off like straws for their drowning occupants. And, of course, some were picked up badly injured.

Harrowing tales, rivalling those which followed in the wake of the Titanic's sinking, came to light as the whole story was pieced together.

Had it not been for the Great War looming up to erase so many earlier tragedies by the sheer, overwhelming number and size of its own, the story of the sinking of the Empress of Ireland would undoubtedly have shared disaster "honours" with Titanic — and the Lusitania, yet to come.

One short interview, among the hundreds which took place as survivors came ashore, epitomised the whole ghastly business of shipwreck. And it came from the lips of a little girl named Helen O'Hara, from Toronto . . . .

Ten-year-old Helen, no doubt tucked snugly into her cot with her favourite doll or teddy, had been awakened by "Papa", who had carried her on deck, whispering soothing words of comfort. Helen had learned to swim at school, and as the ship began to sink and the water lapped around them, she and her father pushed out into the cold darkness.

Her father found a piece of floating wreckage for her to cling to. It wouldn't bear his weight as well. "I did not see papa after that," said Helen.

The youngsters fared worst. Of the 138 children on board, only four survived. Many whole families were wiped out.

The passengers came from many parts of the world, but a high percentage were from Canada, with about 200 from Toronto. Among them was 42-years-old Lawrence Irving, one of the two sons of the late English actor, Sir Henry Irving. Lawrence, also an actor with a promising career, and his wife, actress Mabel Hackney, well known in her own right, were returning from Canada from a successful tour which had ended in Winnipeg the previous week-end. Another notable name on the passenger list was that of Sir Henry Seton-Karr, a Scot born in India, who married into the wealthy glass-manufacturing family of the Pilkington's, of St. Helens, Lancashire. Sir Henry was parliamentary representative for St. Helens for 20 years.

The Irvings, said a witness, were last seen clasped in each other's arms as the ship slid under the water. Sir Henry, once a tough sportsman and explorer, died a gentleman — in evening dress.

As the harvest of nameless dead was gleaned from the sea and eventually brought into Quebec, that city, and Liverpool, too, became cities of sorrow. For a week, mothers, fathers, husbands, wives, sweethearts and friends, walked ashen-faced up and down the long aisles of bodies in their grim searches for loved ones.

Back on Merseyside, the grief was equally strong, for here lived so many of the liner's crew. For scores of families the shipwreck meant not only the irreparable loss of loved ones, but breadwinners, too. A memorial service was held in St. Peter's Church, Church Street, Liverpool (demolished in 1923 and the site of which was occupied by Woolworth's, who opened their first store in Britain in Liverpool). Many women collapsed on this sad occasion.

One of the congregation was a Mrs. Steede, widow of the Empress of Ireland's chief officer, Mr. M. Steede, who had stood a good chance of being saved as he was a strong swimmer. Although how he actually met his death is still a mystery, it seems almost certain that he was crushed by a lifeboat. Mr. Mansfield Steede, of Liverpool, told me this when he was 74. He had attended that service as a lad of ten.

But there was joy for some in Liverpool when, on June 10, 1914, 72 crew survivors arrived home on Merseyside by train from Glasgow, where they had been landed by the Allan Liner, Corsican. Several thousand people massed to greet them. They couldn't all have been relatives and friends. But, in such a collective spirit is how the citizens of Liverpool have always turned out, whether it be for a winning or losing football team, or sorrowful occasions like this, which called for one's presence, if only simply to stand in humble tribute.

Tugs, ferries and other small craft took thousands of sightseers out to see the ships inspected by King George V and Queen Mary on their visit to Merseyside, July 11, 1913, when, on board the Galatea, they opened the new Gladstone Graving Dock. Empress of Ireland (centre) is anchored in mid river.

(Canadian Pacific)

73

As most of these particular survivors had been working in the liner's stokehold and engine-room, they were very fortunate men. Among them was William Clarke, a stoker, who bore a charmed life. Two years earlier, he had also escaped from the bowels of the Titanic.

The captains and crews of other liners, like White Star's Teutonic and the Megantic, paid their own respects by dropping wreaths over the spot where the Empress had sunk.

For many years there has been controversy about the Titanic's band playing "Nearer My God To Thee," as that liner was sinking. But I wonder if this may not have originated from the fact that the Salvation Army band on board the Cunarder Alaunia, actually played this particular hymn? Alaunia was on her way to Liverpool on the return leg of her maiden voyage to Canada. As she passed over the wreck of the Empress of Ireland, the bandmaster dropped a wreath over the side. Among the dead was his mother . . . .

Whose fault was this terrible collision? The blame fell into the lap of Captain Andersen. Storstad had ported her helm in the fog, coming directly across the track of the Empress, it was said. Captain Kendall was exonerated, although, he was advised, he might have been wiser in giving the collier a wider berth.

In the ensuing Great War, Kendall became a commodore of convoys and it was his proud boast that he brought 196 ships safely home. Later, he was appointed a Younger Brother of Trinity House and was Canadian Pacific's marine superintendent in Southampton and in London. Captain Kendall retired in 1939 and lived until he was 91. He died in a London nursing home on November 28, 1965.

Relics from the Empress of Ireland, recovered by divers in July, 1964, included her bell, a quadrant and a 7-ton anchor. These are now in the custody of the Musée Maritime Bernier at Quebec.

Echoes of the tragedy remained until as later as 1965, the year of Kendall's death, when the Empress of Ireland Fund for Dependants was finally closed. But even at the time of writing (1986), there are folk living by the St. Lawrence and the Mersey who still mourn dear ones lost that terrible night.

Footnote:
Coincidentally, colliers were involved in two other collisions with Canadian Pacific liners in the St. Lawrence.

On July 27, 1912, Empress of Britain the first (renamed Montroyal in 1924), rammed and sank the collier Helvetia, inward-bound for Montreal in dense fog. For half an hour she was impaled on the liner's bow. No lives were lost and both ships were blamed for the incident.

The other collision, which took place on June 16, 1935, also in fog, involved the 42,000-ton Empress of Britain the second, homeward-bound from Quebec, and the 5,193-ton Newcastle collier, Kafiristan. The collier lost three men. Princess Catherine of Greece was a passenger in the liner at the time.

This newspaper picture, showing the Empress of Ireland leaving Liverpool Landing Stage, was seen by thousands of readers on Merseyside and in North Wales when it was published after the disaster.

Hildebrand, Hilary & Hubert

Although its liners were relatively small compared with most of the giants sailing in and out of Liverpool during the heydays of the ocean-going passenger ships, Booth Line probably had the edge over all other companies for providing really romantic — and adventurous — cruises.

Its robust little liners, like the Hildebrand, the Hilary and the Hubert, made regular sailings from Liverpool. They called at Portugal and Madeira before crossing the Atlantic to Brazil for Belem and the huge Amazon basin, which drains an area nearly as large as Australia. Fast and comfortable, they were latterly indentified by their black hulls, with red boot topping, white superstructure and black funnel carrying the Booth house-flag insignia on each side.

From their decks, thousands of intrepid explorers and missionaries, businessmen, scientists, authors, diplomats, and anyone with the cash and inclination to buy a ticket to broaden their horizons, saw all the breathtaking beauty of the jungle on passage up the Amazon to Manaus — 1,000 miles from the coast and on the Rio Negro tributary.

The brothers Alfred (the founder) and Charles Booth started their steamship service in 1866, when they began trading between Europe and richly-endowed Brazil, with two vessels, the Augustine and the Jerome. A service between New York and Brazil was initiated in 1882. Later, trade was conducted not merely through Manaus, far inland though this was, but also through Iquitos, in Peru-2,000 miles from the mouth of the Amazon and the sea — via a "feeder" service of shallow-draught vessels.

Iquitos is only about 500 miles from the Pacific Ocean, as the crow flies, but the mighty Andes range, standing between that port and the sea is virtually impassable. So, many imports for Iquitos itself were often shipped from the nearby Pacific Port of Callaos all the way to Liverpool, transhipped and dispatched back to the Amazon — almost to their starting point!

The Amazon and its tributaries were the great highways of Brazil. One of the latter, the Madeira, carried the first "mosquito-proof" steamer — Booth's Vincent (1910-1933). Passengers and crews had sailed on this river before but only at the cost of death and sickness. But the Vincent's two experimental voyages were made with no incident of sickness of any kind.

Having carried cargoes of Brazil nuts, rubber, timber, hides, cotton and countless other tropical items to Europe for more than half a century, the company decided after the Great War to open up the glorious sights of the Amazon to holidaymakers. Booth's had already introduced tours to Lisbon and Madeira way back in 1903, but on June 2, 1922, the company launched the first of four proposed six-week cruises to the world's greatest river, via its passenger liner, Hildebrand (II). Ports of call were Oporto, Lisbon, Madeira, Ceara, Belem and Manaus.

From Belem, the steamers entered a luxuriant stretch of the river, no wider than the Thames at Maidenhead, and known as the Region of a Thousand Islands. Dense vegetation lined the banks within a few yards of the sides of the ships. And that was but a tenth of the river journey, which took one through scenes of unsurpassed beauty in tropical flora and fauna.

Hildebrand (II) began the cruises which took passengers into the heart of the world's greatest "garden" – the Amazonian forests. She carried many famous personalities. (Booth Steamship Company)

Some newcomers sailing through this jungle paradise in the old days would take pot-shots from the decks at the creatures of the forest, but this practice was rightfully stopped. Indians also walked along those banks!

Manaus, the big river port of the interior, virtually carved out of the jungle, even today still displays evidence of its rubber-boom years in fine roads and buildings, including a domed opera house!

Using the steamer as a convenient and comfortable hotel, passengers on these special cruises were able to join little expeditions from Manaus to see the primeval forest at first hand by exploring creeks overhung with lush foliage and highly coloured blooms; birds with gorgeous plumage and big, bright butterflies. They had the opportunity of stealing through the virgin forest to the Taruma Falls, and a stern-wheeler would be chartered for the river expeditions.

Boats from the latter went into the flooded, dense undergrowth, from which mighty trees thrust their heads to mingle with the mosses and lianas, which created another jungle in the sky. These meandering waterways, concealing alligators, deadly water-snakes, electric eels, stingrays and shoals of voracious piranha fish, were often overgrown to the extent that oars could not be used and tree trunks and branches afforded the means of propulsion. Another interesting trip arranged was that to see the giant and colourful Victoria Regia water-lilies, growing in profusion in the still creeks.

Many of the cruise passengers returned to Liverpool with souvenir orchids growing from small, mossy logs, which they hung in their cabins during the voyage.

However, passengers like the genuine explorers and the missionaries, who used the liner service to this wild and then still-unspoiled vast area of the world, pushed off deep into often unknown territory, veined with numerous rivers, where savage headhunters awaited the unwary. Some never returned . . . !

The fares for these cruises in the 1920's originally ranged from £80 to £100, but with the ensuring depression, these dropped considerably. In April, 1933, for example, the complete all-in cruise, including ports of call and the shore excursions, cost but £55. . . a concessionary rate because the fare had been reduced from £75.

Hildebrand II, a graceful, single-funnelled twin-screw steamer of 6,995 tons, built by Scott's of Greenock, in 1911, made many of these 14,000-mile round voyages from Liverpool and was a great favourite among her regular passengers, some of whom were famous people. At the time of her launching, she was called "the electric and mosquito-proof ship". The Journal of Commerce of February 1, 1912, recalled "that a good many of the illustrious names associated with the history of Liverpool were to be found on her passenger list when, after completing her maiden voyage, she took a large party to Spithead to honour King George V at the Coronation Naval Review."

During the Great War, stripped of her finery, this liner became a very efficient and useful unit of the 10th Cruiser Squadron of Armed Merchantmen. In her three years' service, she stopped some 500 vessels for examination of their papers. One of the vessels she "arrested" and sent into port under escort, carried an American millionaire who, at the time, was bound for Stockholm in a noble but wild attempt to stop the war.

On another occasion, by means of her wireless, the Hildebrand was also instrumental in the capture of four suspect spies. For the latter part of the war she acted as a convoy escort.

Hildebrand herself was stopped once, too. In 1924, much to her passengers' dismay, she had to curtail a trip up the Amazon because of a revolution in Brazil. She went to Barbados instead. She continued in this service until 1932 and was laid up at Milford Haven in July that year.

When the chairman, Mr. Charles Booth, in January, 1934, deemed her no longer suitable for cruising, Hildebrand was sold to the Bristol Channel shipbreakers for £10,000.

Hildebrand II's "Amazon" sister was the 7,402-ton liner, Hilary, which carried on the name of her two earlier sisters. The second of these, built in 1907, was lost in World War 1, while in service with the 10th Cruiser Squadron. An awesome story is told about her sinking after being torpedoed off Ushant in May, 1917.

Way below the surface, she exploded with tremendous force. She obviously disturbed one of the unknown denizens of the deep, for a huge serpent suddenly reared out of the sea and absolutely terrified the already-distressed survivors who were then in the lifeboats. This story is not simply a sailor's yarn, for it was verified by Commander A.J. Bell, D.S.C., R.N.R., one of those survivors, and also by the commander and some of the crew of the U.boat which sank the Hilary.

Nine of the 11 requisitioned Booth ships were lost in the Great War.

Hilary the third made a notable addition to the Booth Line fleet when built by Cammell Laird's in 1931. She made her maiden voyage from Liverpool to Manaus on August 14 that year carrying 80 first-class passengers in single-berth cabins on the promenade-deck, with single, double and a few three-berth cabins on the upper deck.

The long-lived Hilary (III), the first British liner to return to Manaus, a thousand miles up the Amazon, after the last war. She was once the subject of a "nightmare" event. (Booth Steamship Company)

Provision was also made for 250 third-class passengers. Her complement included Mr. Booth and his family, on passage to Madeira.

This liner had trouble in the tricky Amazon twice in her early years. She ran aground 170 miles below Manaus in November, 1935, and again, two miles east of Goiabel the following April. But more serious was the occasion when she ran on to rocks near Holyhead, Anglesey, in dense fog on Easter Sunday, April 9, 1939.

Bound for Liverpool via the Canary Islands, after the usual cruise to Brazil, she struck the rocks of isolated Carmel Head at 12.45 a.m. Because of the fog, it was several hours before help arrived. While Holyhead lifeboat was searching for her, another life-saving crew, travelling as far as possible by road, had to abandon their lorry and cross fields, walls and hedges with heavy apparatus before they reached the stricken liner. The Frazerburgh trawler, Dewy Rose, also assisted.

Although the liner had sprung a leak forward, there was no panic and her 100 and more passengers were taken off safely. But it was an unfortunate experience for her master, Captain Lewis Evans, of Pwllheli, who was due to retire after that voyage. The Hilary was later refloated and taken in tow to Liverpool.

More at home in the heat of South America, Hilary (III) lies at her Liverpool berth alongside a wintry quay. (Booth Steamship Company)

Above:
Guides take a party of passengers for a boat trip among the giant water lilies. Note the fashions of the 'Twenties!

Below:
Hilary (III) steams up the placid waters of the Amazonian Narrows.

Above:
Close-up of the biggest flowers in the world . . . Victoria Regia water lilies growing in the creeks of the Amazon.

Below:
What lurks in the waters of these tropical glades? Cruise passengers survey the jungle!

Above:
Cool wicker chairs and tables furnish the smoking room in Hildebrand (II).

Below:
When King Neptune rules supreme! . . . just one act from the many "Crossing-the-Line" ceremonies enacted on the Booth Line steamers.

Passengers, at ease on Hildebrand's promenade deck, take in the beauty of the jungle-clad banks and riverside villages of the mighty Amazon.

Hilary was the first British liner to return to Manaus after the last war and, back home at Liverpool, in March, 1947, she brought news of many of the Amazonian Indian tribes fast dying out from epidemics of influenza.

In June, 1953, she ran aground again in the Amazon — on the same notorious Mandahy Bank, which had held her fast in April, 1936. That was quite an adventurous voyage. A small tug, trying to refloat the liner, overturned and sank, and her chief engineer had his leg fractured in three places when hit by the tug's propellers. Hilary's boat was lowered and four of the tug's crew were picked out of the fast-flowing river. Then the injured engineer was spotted.

With true British grit, the liner's surgeon, Dr. Kenneth Wood, of Tynemouth, dived in to the rescue, gripping in his teeth a morphia-loaded syringe to deaden the man's severe pain. Helped by Mr. Albert Martin, a fireman with Hilary, of Everton, Liverpool, he brought the wounded man to safety. Both rescuers, who braved the turbid, death-concealing water, earned the plaudits of passengers and crew. Eventually, they were awarded the Bronze Medal and Certificate of the Liverpool Shipwreck and Humane Society for their courageous action.

Hilary did her stint of last-war service and was requisitioned by the Admiralty in January, 1941, firstly as an ocean boarding-vessel.

In March, 1943, she was fitted out as an infantry-landing ship and took part in the invasion of Sicily as the headquarters vessel of Rear-Admiral Sir Philip Vian. Commodore G.N. Oliver flew his pennant from the Hilary at the Salerno landings in December, when he commanded the Northern Attack Force. Later, in July, 1944, she was in action again, at the D-Day landings in Normandy, when Admiral Vian transferred his flag to her. Reconditioned in 1945, she returned to the Amazon run once more.

The Hilary was involved in a frightening incident in December, 1956, when on her way home from West Africa, via Las Palmas, on charter to Elder Dempster. Two days out of Freetown, at midnight on December 5, she went out of control. An 18-inch wheel-key was found jammed in her steering gear. For 20 minutes, the liner drifted helplessly in a busy sea-lane, with 170 passengers on board, most of them enjoying a carnival dance. Her master at this time, Captain Tom Williams, decribed this event as "a nightmare".

Police boarded the liner at Liverpool. Sabotage, at first suspected, was ruled out after a five-day investigation. The jamming was thought to have been caused accidentally.

Hilary was scrapped in 1960.

Hildebrand (III) was fated to live a short life for a ship. She made her maiden voyage from Liverpool to Brazil in December, 1951, and was wrecked off Portugal in September, 1957. (Booth Steamship Company)

The stern half of the wrecked Hildebrand is lashed by a heavy swell as she lies fast aground some 18 miles from Lisbon. (Booth Steamship Company)

Hildebrand the third, a 7,735-ton passenger-cargo liner, was launched at Cammell Laird's on July 20, 1951, as the first Booth Line ship to be built there since 1935. A single-screw ship, accommodating 40 first-class passengers on the upper and promenade decks, and 120 tourist-class, she made her maiden voyage from Liverpool to Brazil on December 28, 1951, to maintain a service between the Mersey and the Amazon, via Portugal, Madeira, Tenerife and Manaus. Captain (later Fleet Commodore) Jackson Whayman, an old Conway, who had served with Booth Line for 30 years, and whose father, Captain W.R. Whayman, was a master for 20 years, took this command.

One of the four Liverpool ships which took part in the 1953 Coronation Review at Spithead (the others were the Samaria, the Patroclus and the Alca), Hildebrand was fated to live only about a quarter of her namesake's (Hildebrand II) life, for she came to grief on September 25, 1957. Outward-bound from Liverpool for North Brazil, via the West Indies, she went aground in fog near Cascais, about 18 miles from Lisbon and at the mouth of the River Tagus. Some 160 passengers were disembarked by tugs and no one was hurt, but Hildebrand, with a gaping hole in her bow and two holds and the engine-room flooded, was doomed.

Her master, Captain Thomas E. Williams, and crew remained on board for days while tugs endeavoured to refloat her, but Hildebrand was stuck fast. Eventually abandoned and her cargo, valued at £1 million, removed, she became a total loss.

Hildebrand's sister ship, the 7,800-ton Hubert (also the third, and built by Cammell Laird's) was launched on August 31, 1954. She had accommodation for 74 first-class passengers and 96 tourist-class. Like her sister, she also had fine staterooms and facilities especially planned to suit the climatic conditions encountered on her tropical voyages.

Rather like the Hilary's experience of River Amazon rescues, in July, 1953, the Hubert was involved in a similar incident at Fortaleza, North Brazil, on September 8, 1964. Greaser James Healy, of Bootle, fell into shark-infested waters as he tried to climb on board the ship, and his colleague, ship's carpenter Bryan McNamara, dived to his rescue. Bryan also received the Liverpool Shipwreck and Humane Society's medal for bravery.

In 1964, the Hubert was renamed Malaysia and went to the Austasia Line of Singapore.

* * *

The 7,800-ton Hubert (III), launched in August, 1954, was sold 10 years later and renamed Malaysia.

Recalling ships which have gone aground on mud-banks and sand-spits, and the difficulties of navigation in rivers and estuaries like the Amazon, reminds me of an amusing tale told about the famous author and river-pilot, Mark Twain.

As a Mississippi paddle-boat pilot, Mark was once asked by a woman passenger if he was the man who knew where all the sandbanks were.

"No, ma'am," he replied. "I'm the man who knows where they ain't!"

* * *

Before closing this chapter on the romantic Booth Line (taken over by the Vestey Group in 1946), worthy of note, I think, is the comment made by Mr. R.L. Hichens, the chairman of Cammell Laird's, on the occasion of the launching of the S.S. Hilary on April 17, 1931. Talking about the depressed state of shipping and shipbuilding, he forecast improvement. He said that people would still want to travel by ships and thought that the aeroplane would never replace the ship.

Yet, during the war, in November, 1943, it was announced that the Booth Steamship Company, with four other important British shipping lines — Blue Star, Royal Mail, P.S.N.C. and Lamport and Holt, all trading with South America — were forming a separate company. This was for the purpose of operating air services between the U.K. and the Continent and South America, as soon as the necessary consents and machines could be obtained.

A year later, the British-Latin America Air Lines Ltd., as this company styled itself, was predicting flights to Rio in little more than 30 hours, compared with seven days pre-war!

Lancastria

The last war took a frightful toll of life at sea and, but for the security restrictions at the time, far greater publicity would have been accorded to the sinking of the Cunarder Lancastria, bombed and sunk off St. Nazaire, France, in 1940, with the loss of 3,000 souls — twice as many as those lost in the Titanic.

Lancastria was not launched under that name. She was originally laid down on Clydeside in March, 1914, as Anchor Line's 16,700-ton passenger liner, Tyrrenhia, when work on her was stopped following the outbreak of the Great War. The Cunard Steamship Company took her over after the war to help make up its tonnage, diminished by enemy action, and Tyrrenhia made her maiden voyage, under that name, from Glasgow to Canada on June 13, 1922.

As a passenger liner on the Liverpool-Quebec-Montreal run, she did not make a great hit among transatlantic travellers. Many, in fact, had difficulty in pronouncing and spelling her name. So, in February, 1924, the year after she had been placed on the Hamburg-Southampton-New York service, she was renamed Lancastria. She worked the London-Havre-Southampton-New York service between 1926 and 1932 and then became a cruising liner, until the outbreak of the last world war when she was converted into a troop transport. After voyages to Norway and Iceland, she was laid up at Liverpool for overhaul and, on June 14, 1940, her officers and crew who had only just been signed off, were hastily recalled to the ship and the morning of June 16 found her under Admiralty orders at Plymouth.

That evening, Lancastria and the Cunarder Franconia, sailed for Brest, a town under fire, for these were the days of Dunkirk, when the British Expeditionary Force was pulling out of France, with the Germans close behind. As things were too hot at Brest, the ships were ordered to move on down the coast to Quiberon Bay and St. Nazaire, to join several other big vessels awaiting the fleeing hordes of troops and civilians racing for the coast and evacuation from the big port.

Former Liverpool crewman, Michael Sheehan, now living in Toronto, was at the wheel of Lancastria in the middle watch when he heard the master, Captain Sharp, tell the first officer, Mr. Roberts, that they were making for St. Nazaire. Mike was on board because, while having a drink in Jack Preston's pub in Canning Place, Liverpool, he had heard that Lancastria needed a crew in a hurry. "Naturally, after a pay-off, it would be almost impossible to catch up with all her former crew," he told me . . . .

Shortly after 4 a.m., he turned into his bunk, but very soon German aircraft howled down and sprayed the Lancastria's bridge

Lancastria, formerly the Tyrrenhia. When she was bombed and sunk, the loss of life was twice the number of those who perished in the Titanic.
(Cunard archives, University of Liverpool)

with machine-gun bullets. "About an hour later, they came back, dropping several bombs," he said. "Two dropped close to the Franconia, causing damage in her engine-room and she had to return to Plymouth. We carried on alone, arriving at St. Nazaire about 7.30 a.m., when we dropped both anchors. No sooner were we secured than the loading of troops and many civilians, including women and children, began.

"About 11 a.m., a group of enemy planes attacked. These missed us but got the Oronsay with a direct hit on her bridge. Meanwhile, we loaded a large contingent of Air Force personnel into No.2 hatch in the lower hold. There must have been close to a thousand of those unfortunate men in that hold. They had little space to move around and were packed like sardines."

He was back on watch at noon and was "handed a gadget to keep track of the number of people coming on board." At 2 p.m., he reported to the first officer a figure of well over 4,000, which didn't include the crew. "There was hardly any space in which to move on the ship," he said, and recalled a conversation among the captain and senior officers, in which it was agreed that the ship could not cope with any more occupants. These were still pouring on board when Mike was told to notify the gangway officer that, after a destroyer had finished discharging her load of passengers, the gangway was to be taken in.

Mike went back to the bridge and the wheel, believing that Lancastria was about to get under way. "Not so," he said. "The Captain was insisting on waiting for an escort as we had been getting attacked all day. There is no doubt in my mind that Captain Sharp had a very tough decision to make. At least we had anti-aircraft fire from the destroyer and other ships, and whatever Bren-gun and rifle fire that could be set up around us. But we were a sitting duck."

90

Although an elegant liner on the transatlantic run, few passengers enthused over the Lancastria. However, there is little doubt that her dining room here saw some magnificent meals presented. (Cunard archives)

Mike Sheehan said that he found the utmost difficulty in threading his way through the carpet of troops on the decks. There was hardly space for them to sit or stretch out and they were continually under attack. "I guess that they were so tired and exhausted that they didn't give a damn one way or the other," he said.

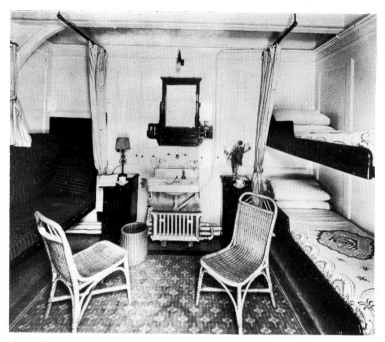

A tourist stateroom in the Lancastria, as this looked in March, 1932.
(Cunard archives)

"The first bomb got us — down into No.2 hatch among all the Air Force men," he said. "If any of them ever got out, the only chance they would have had was by the rope ladders, rigged for that purpose. For myself, I didn't know what had hit me. The explosion threw me way up the fore end of the working alley, landing me a short distance from the forward scuttle. The lamp-trimmer was lying across the entrance. He had been hit and I helped to move him on to the deck as everyone was scrambling over him to get out. The Chief Officer told Bosun Billy Hayden to get his gang to swing out the starboard lifeboats, and they had just started to do this when the next air attack came.

"The Chief Officer and I managed to duck behind the bridge rail, but Mr.Roberts, the First Officer, didn't make it in time. He and the bosun were killed. A few minutes later, another attack was made, with the aircraft flying not much higher than the foremast. That was when a bomb fell down one of Lancastria's funnels. I understand that one fell on the foredeck, too.

"Lancastria started going down by the head and there was some commotion. Most people seemed to be in a state of shock and many were scrambling to get into the starboard boats before they were properly swung out. The deck-gang had quite a job on hand as falls were getting jammed. The Chief Officer and I were still hanging on to the bridge rail, finding it increasingly difficult to keep our feet. The next thing I knew was being on the foredeck. I cut off all my clothes and jumped over the side, striking out for the nearest thing afloat, which was a hatch-board. A couple of soldiers joined me and we managed to get clear of the ship. She was going down fast. Her bunker-oil was released and spreading all over the water. We couldn't escape it. At the same time, the bastards were machine-gunning us and dropping incendiaries to try and set fire to the floating oil.

"The two soldiers with me were hit in one of these attacks and they died. The last I saw of the ship was a sorrowful sight, with three-quarters of her fore-end under and her stern and propellers in the air. I was feeling so damn cold and was covered with oil. A French tug then came along, moving through a lot of us and making no attempt to pick anyone up. Then our Spitfires came and put the Jerries to flight. This encouraged us and soon I was picked up by the minesweeper HMS Cambridgeshire, which later transferred a

Lancastria at Capetown in the early 1930's.　　　　(Cunard archives)

number of us to the S.S. Robert C. Holt. This ship was also loaded with survivors, many of whom were badly wounded and didn't make Plymouth.

"We arrived at Plymouth in a couple of days, late at night, but it seemed that the whole town was out there on the dock waiting to look after us. They did a great job, and today, all this time afterwards, I would still like to express my gratitude and appreciation to those wonderful people of Plymouth who just couldn't do enough for us. From then on, the Cunard Company took over and we were taken by train back to Liverpool, where we were paid off."

★ ★ ★ ★ ★

Liverpool flyweight boxer, Joe Curran, who had joined the Merchant Navy, was another Lancastria survivor. A fireman, his hands were badly burned when he slid down a rope from the sinking ship into the sea and he was in the water for one and a half hours before being rescued. Yet, a few days later, Joe was back in the ring at the Liverpool Stadium fighting, as a substitute, Jimmy Lyden, who knocked him out after six rounds. The crowd hadn't a clue what a hell the young boxer had been through.

Mr. Joseph Parry, of Hollywood, County Down, Northern Ireland, was serving with the Royal Army Medical Corps in France at the time of the mass evacuation. He and others were picked up from a quayside at St. Nazaire by the destroyer, Havoc, and transferred to a French tug, under British command, which took them alongside the Lancastria.

"She was packed from stem to stern and we were unable to board her," he told me. "We then proceeded towards the P & O liner, Oronsay, lying about half a mile away. Half way between the vessels all hell let loose and the bombs fell. We saw two bombs hit the Lancastria, the first forward and the second appeared to go straight down a funnel. She took about 17 minutes to sink from sight, according to our timing."

Joe and his mates obtained permission to lower a lifeboat from the tug. They took one boatload of survivors to a destroyer and two more loads (towing a liferaft in addition) to their tug. "Later," he said, "we managed to get them all aboard the Oronsay, whose catering staff had turned a large saloon into a sick-bay. Our total was 239 survivors and 111 casualties, which included 65 lying-cases, the remainder walking-wounded. We eventually arrived at Plymouth, where the Royal Navy's medical staff came out in ambulance-barges to take off the lying wounded, whom we helped carry down the gangway on the ship's side."

Mike Sheehan and Joe Curran were but two men of many thousands involved in the Lancastria-bombing. Other survivors have told me similar stories of how she was bombed and, how in a nightmare of bawled orders and the screams of the injured and dying, she sank so quickly. It was every man, woman and child for himself, but sadly, not all had the same chance of survival. Many were killed outright by the blasts and some died as victims of burns and bullets. Others were trapped below.

Some 3,000 died in that morass of blood, oil and splintered ship, which was one of the greatest sea disasters ever recorded. Master of the Lancastria on her last grim voyage, Captain Sharp, of Wallasey, Merseyside, survived that holocaust only to die in the torpedoed liner, Laconia, two years later.

*Commander R. Sharp, of Wallasey...
thrown off Lancastria's bridge as she
sank and spent four hours in the
water.*

*Liverpool's former world flyweight
title contender, Joe Curran died in
1984, aged 70.* (Gordon Whiting)

Mauretania the Second

Although she never matched her predecessor (in my opinion, the most romantic liner of all time), Mauretania the Second still became a ship which won the admiration of North Atlantic travellers and cruise passengers.

Because she was built at Cammell Laird's Birkenhead, she was very much "a child of the Mersey," particularly endeared to Merseysiders, who also called her "Maurie" as they did the legendary ship whose name she bore.

From his office suite in the dignified Cunard Building on Liverpool's waterfront, Cunard White Star's chairman, Sir Percy Bates, virtually watched her growing across the river as she lay on No.6 slipway, previously occupied by the famous aircraft carrier, Ark Royal. Her neighbour was the huge battleship, Prince of Wales.

Mauretania's keel plates were laid on Empire Day, May 24, 1937. Then just plain No.1029, she was to become, at 35,738 tons, the largest ship ever to be built in England. Strangely, the liner was only the third Cunarder to be built in the company's own backyard, as it

A fine night study of Mauretania tied up at Prince's Landing Stage, Liverpool, in December, 1953.

were. Scotland's shipyards seemed to be favoured with Cunard's orders and, up till then, Laird's had built only the Cephalania in 1882 and the Samaria (1920) for Cunard. Even so, Mauretania's lifeboats were still constructed at Renfrew!

The two biggest gear-wheels in any liner up to that time — 46 feet in circumference, 15ft. in diameter, with 7ft. rims, weighing 85 tons each and forged by Harland and Wolff at Govan — were so large that they had to be brought round the coast instead of overland.

It took nearly three months of day and night work to cut the teeth of these wheels, which transmitted the power of the liner's turbines to the propeller shafts.

After keeping the public in suspense for months, Cunard White Star, in October, 1937, announced the liner's name, thus reviving that which had been made internationally famous by Mauretania the first. The name had been carefully preserved. Back in January, 1936, while old Maurie was being broken up, Mr. C.J. Sharp, the chairman of the Southampton and Isle of Wight Steam Packet Company, announced that his company's little paddle-steamer, Queen (350 tons), would be renamed Mauretania "to oblige the Cunard Company".

"We shall hold the name until they want it again, and then we shall surrender it," he said. So, little 'Maurie', busy paddling down Bournemouth way, became the Corfe Castle on Mauretania's launching day.

Rudderless and tug-assisted, Maurie the second made her first "voyage" across the Mersey from Birkenhead to Bootle, on May 14, 1939. (H.A. Smith)

To commemorate this special day, the paddle-steamer's master and crew sent this telegram: "On the day of your baptism, your diminutive stepsister sends greetings and cordial good wishes for a long and famous career."

Maurie's launching, on sunny July 28, 1938, was probably the most spectacular launch ever seen on the Mersey, and she also made British shipyard history in that the 27 inch-high brass letters, emblazoned on her bow, were unveiled as a tribute to the old Mauretania. Some 50,000 shipyard workers, relatives and officials, watched Lady Bates, the chairman's wife, name the ship with the traditional bottle of champagne, then press a button to unveil the name, until then draped with the Union Flag and the Stars and Stripes. Lady Bates, who died in 1973, aged 93, was the grand-daughter of Charles MacIver, virtual founder of the Cunard Line, who had ancestral links with the Vikings. MacIver introduced the red and green navigation lights.

And, perhaps because there was something magic in the name Mauretania, scores of thousands thronged the Mersey's banks to see the new liner glide down the 760ft. slipway, greased with seven tons of tallow. It was indeed a joyous occasion, except for one poor fellow. Robert Johnston, a 35-years-old paraplegic, had propelled himself in

Entering Gladstone Graving Dock and sailing over her 45-ton rudder (lying on the dock bottom) waiting to be fitted when the dock was drained.

a wheel-chair from Hull to Liverpool to see the launch — and then missed it by only minutes. He had taken nearly a week to make the 130-mile trip, only to be held up by a goods train at Queen's Dock.

Unlike her predecessor at her Tyneside launch, Mauretania II needed no drag chains to restrain her. The river at that point of launching is a mile wide and, except for eight attentive tugs standing by, shipping was warned off by maroons. She gathered speed as the band played "Rule Britannia", and with a burst of cheering from thousands of throats, sirens and klaxons blaring, roaring aircraft dipping in salute, Maurie splashed down in a cascade of driftwood from her cradle.

Some 7,000 men built Mauretania and before she was completed, she gave employment to 150,000 people in a hundred cities and towns. So popular was her name that seven months before her launch, 500 passengers had booked accommodation for her maiden voyage. She would accommodate 1,500 passengers in cabin, tourist and third-classes, and she was called a sunshine palace of glass and gold. No luxury was spared and she even boasted three cinemas.

"She is a floating repository of 20th Century wonders," enthused the Liverpool Echo, a month before her launch. "Her wireless communications system, sound-reproduction system, directional-finding and deep-sea sounding apparatus all embody the very latest results of research." And, of course, these did, just a little more than a year before the war which was to make such wonders commonplace, and greatly improve upon them, too.

Said another journal at that time: "Radio telegrams may be sent to England and America and messages to other ships simultaneously, and from public kiosks near the lifts, passengers may talk by telephone to any subscriber in the world without noise or interference. The volume of music broadcast in the big public rooms — a relay of the ship's orchestra, records, or a wireless programme — will be regulated according to the number of people in the room. Two or three of the loudspeakers in the restaurant are inside the hollow pillars and others are concealed in various parts of the ship. Science has stepped in again to prevent interference with her sound reproduction system from the ship's lighting and power, which is almost sufficient to run a large town's service . . . ."

Yes, these, too, were big advances in an age where thousands of folk still installed unsightly aerials in their backyards to hear their favourite "wireless" programmes through a sea of oscillation and background hissing from their large and clumsy sets.

The great liner's 25-ton manganese-bronze twin propellers gave her 26 knots. Although about 3,800 tons heavier and 67 feet longer than the old Maurie, but with the same breadth, she was not built to capture Blue Riband records. Probably the first thing that people noticed about the new ship was that she looked entirely different from her four-funnelled predecessor because she had only two funnels. And, although more speed records were anticipated from a ship which bore such a famous name, she was in fact built simply as an intermediate liner and not an ocean-going yacht built for speed.

An interesting feature of this liner was that her huge funnels were not encumbered with external steam-pipes, and this gave them a "cleaner" and more streamlined look.

Among British merchant ships she rated about fifth in size and twelfth in the world. Total height from keel to the highest part of her superstructure, incorporating 10 decks, was 111 feet 2 inches with her foremast rising 211 feet above the keel. Her holds could accept 390,000 cubic feet of cargo and she also had accommodation for 70 cars. Her hull was sub-divided into 37 watertight compartments and she carried 24 lifeboats.

Maurie's 45-ton rudder, with an overall width of 19 feet 6 inches was transported to the shipyard by what was then the world's biggest lorry — a 100-ton vehicle owned by Edward Box and Company, of Speke, Liverpool. This lorry had quite a reputation and children would often gather to see it along the routes it took. Because of heavy snow (December, 1938), the lorry took a week to deliver the rudder from Darlington to Merseyside and was held up for days on the moorland Woodhead Pass, while men had to dig it out and clear a path. In the best of conditions, this lorry travelled at only 5 m.p.h. and was followed by a cyclist carrying a red flag!

Well-known British artists contributed to the internal decor of the Mauretania, and it was fitting that a Merseyside painter, Winifred O. Humphreys, should be among them. Miss Humphreys, a scene-painter and designer at the Liverpool Playhouse, painted circus subjects on white sycamore panels of the liner's children's playroom. One of the most striking decorations in the public rooms was designed by Cameron Baillie, of the Slade School — a bas-relief carving featuring the North Atlantic bridged by the two Mauretanias.

Maurie No.2 made her first "voyage", rudderless and tug-assisted, four miles up the Mersey and across to Bootle to be dry-docked in the Gladstone Dock system. Few spectators watched this event, starting at 7 a.m. on the cold, wet day of May 14, 1939. She actually sailed over her great rudder, lying at the bottom of the graving dock in readiness to be fitted, when some 44,000,000 gallons of water was emptied from the dock.

Appropriately, her master on her trials — which took place in the Firth of Clyde — was Captain A.T. Brown, of Scarborough, the last captain of the old Mauretania, which he took to Rosyth for breaking up. The pilot was Mr. J. Lawley. Among the privileged passengers on this trip were Sir Percy Bates, Cunard's chairman, and Mr. Robert S. Johnson, the managing director of Cammell Laird's.

The new Mauretania leaving Gladstone Dock lock, Merseyside, for her trials in the Firth of Clyde. (D.P. & E.)

Those were trials that Mr. Johnson would never forget. He could have been on board the submarine Thetis, built by his yard at Birkenhead, which sank on her trials in Liverpool Bay on June 1, 1939. Only four of the complement of 103 officers, crew, shipyard workers and other observers escaped. Mr. Johnson had been on every other Cammell Laird-built submarine since he became managing director. How fortunate for him that he chose the liner's trials.

Many who remember this disaster felt at that time that somehow this seemed to be a curtain-raiser to the war, only three months off. The tragedy took the warmth out of the sun over Merseyside. Thetis was later salvaged and recommissioned as the Thunderbolt, and had a successful war record, including sinking the Italian submarine, Tarantine, in the Bay of Biscay in 1940. She herself was finally torpedoed in the Mediterranean in 1943, while on convoy work, with the loss of 62 lives . . . .

Maurie was proudly led out of the Mersey, to Liverpool Bay and the deep sea at last, by Skirmisher, Cunard's tender and Merseyside's oldest ship at 55 years. It was Skirmisher which attended the old Mauretania on her maiden voyage.

Among the ships Captain Brown had commanded were those with the famous names of Saxonia, Lancastria, Franconia, Aquitania and Britannic. And, like most sailors, he could tell some good yarns.

101

Some of these concerned his younger days in sail, in which he had served for nine years. His first ship was the Arabella, a little barque of 600 tons.

"We went round the world in her," he said before the Maurie went off on her trials. "We could hoist her on to our bridge (Mauretania's bridge). Good heavens, I should be afraid to go outside the Mersey in her today!"

One of Captain Brown's tales is not for the squeamish. He used to tell how he sailed on one voyage as a cadet in a barque filled with rats. They were carrying a cargo of guano, collected from an island in the South Seas, and soon this began to give off ammonia fumes, which sent the rats topside. These fought refuge everywhere — even in the tops. "One morning — and this is perfectly true," said Captain Brown, "I awoke to find my finger-nails and my toe-nails had been nibbled down almost to the quicks while I slept. I told the skipper and all he said was: 'Well, you must be a young sleepy-head.' But by the next morning, every man in the ship had been 'manicured' by rats!"

With experiences like that in mind, the clean, comfortable and ratless cabin that Captain Brown occupied when Maurie No.2 sped down the famous Skelmorlie Mile within the Admiralty-measured distance off the Isle of Arran, must have seemed like a palace to him.

The Mauretania passed her trials with flying colours, and although her contract speed was set at 23 knots, it was stated on her return from Scotland that she was capable of 26 knots.

Crowds watch on the Wallasey shoreline as Mauretania (II), dressed overall, gathers speed near the Mersey estuary as she starts her maiden voyage to New York on June 17, 1939.

At an inaugural luncheon on board the liner, dressed gaily overall and "at home" in Gladstone Dock, the Lord Mayor of Liverpool said that the city rejoiced that Mauretania bore upon her stern the name of Liverpool, for the admiration of New York and the admonition of London!

Sir Percy Bates spoke of "living in a difficult world, and the difficulty is more acutely felt in this business of ours, a link between Europe and America, than in almost any other. Our voyage figures are almost as good a barometer as the Stock Exchange of what men are thinking and wondering as to the past, present and, more especially, the future."

More than 6,000 people inspected the liner as she lay in the Bootle dock and, with 5,000 sixpenny souvenir medals, made from the metal of the old Mauretania, it was expected to raise £1,000 for the Thetis Relief Fund.

The new Mauretania said farewell to Liverpool on her maiden voyage at 7.15 p.m. on June 17, 1939, when she left the landing stage to the cheers of thousands of spectators. She had been lying in the river since 11.30 that morning and had anchored until about 3 p.m. when she came alongside the stage for passenger embarkation. This was a grand river spectacle, with the Reina del Pacifico, dressed overall, also alongside and George's and Prince's stages completely occupied by various vessels.

Among the passengers were the first-class ticket-holders, Mr. and Mrs. Robert Stevenson Middlemass, of Glasgow, who had travelled in the first Mauretania on her maiden voyage. Film star Ray Milland was another, and Stuart Robinson, the operatic, radio and concert singer, and Arthur Shields, of the Abbey Theatre, Dublin, going to the U.S. to make the film "Drums Along The Mohawk". And, of course, hundreds more who, like the 40 members of the Junior Car Club, heading for the special rally in America, were also going to visit the World's Fair at New York.

Aircraft flew over the liner and dipped in salute to her, and scores of sailing boats made a picturesque background for this grand start to her maiden voyage. More poignant, perhaps, than all the flamboyant trappings of the bon-voyage, was the sound of bells pealing their special God-speed from the ancient "Sailors' Church" of Our Lady and St.Nicholas, on the historic site which had seen the birth of Liverpool nearly a thousand years ago. This peal, which took three hours and thirty-three minutes, and involved 5,007 changes, was composed by Sir A.P. Heywood and conducted by Mr. P.W. Cave.

Several lorry-loads of silver specie was carried by the liner. The total sum was undisclosed but estimated to exceed considerably the £2½ million in gold bullion carried from the Bank of England to the U.S. Treasury by the first Mauretania on her maiden voyage.

Incidentally, the gold trophy awarded to boxer Henry Armstrong, who defeated Ernie Roderick, the Liverpool welterweight, on points, in the championship bout at Harringay on May 25, 1939, was also on board — in the custody of British boxing manager, Ted Broadribb.

Other passengers included Mr. B.K. Klag, chairman of Chrysler and Dodge Motors; Mr. A.R. Cartwright, sales manager, General Motors; Mr. W. Wallace, director of Rowntree's, York and Mr. A. Phillips, chairman of Godfrey Philips, the tobacco manufacturers.

Maurie 2 passed the Mersey Bar lightship at 9 p.m. and arrived at Cobh (Cork), Eire, at 9 a.m. next day for a civic reception at which Captain Brown was presented with a gold medallion inscribed with the arms of the Port of Cork. She left four hours later. Captain Brown then mentioned that the following year, Mauretania would be marking a centenary link between Cork and the Cunard Company, for it was in 1840 that Cunard's pioneer vessels — a quartet of paddle steamers, with accommodation for only 100 passengers, and capable of but $8\frac{1}{2}$ knots — first put into the port of Cork.

Sir Percy Bates said "Howdee" to Mayor La Guardia of New York long before Maurie arrived there. Speaking from the liner at sea, he was exchanging greetings which were broadcast in the States over the Mutual Broadcasting System in their "Welcome, Neighbour," programme. Mayor La Guardia was in Buffalo at the time. The new liner was given a tremendous welcome in New York and large crowds thronged the waterfront as she steamed up the Hudson River in bright sunshine to the shrieking sirens of scores of vessels. Aircraft circled her and the fireboats put on their special water-cascade display.

Mauretania tied up at 2.10 BST. She had taken 6 days, 19 hours. On her return leg to Southampton she took 5 days, 22 hours, 22 minutes from Ambrose Channel lightship to Cherbourg breakwater. Her best day's run was an average of 23.70 knots but, as Captain Brown said: "That is not the highest speed of which she is capable. It was all that was necessary to bring us back on schedule."

If Liverpool and New York had put up a great show of welcome, it seemed nothing compared with that in London, where Mauretania arrived on August 6, as the largest ship ever to sail up the Thames to King George V Dock, her new home berth. An estimated 100,000 spectators lined the banks from Tilbury onwards, shouting good wishes all the way.

Mauretania had a busy war career and, right from the start, the Nazis earmarked her for destruction. Only a month after the declaration of war, a German radio broadcast in English from Hamburg declared that the liner had left New York with only a few passengers and three guns mounted on her decks. Said the announcer: "The British Admiralty will no doubt accept responsibility for this action."

Aerial view of the Mauretania arriving in New York at the end of her maiden voyage and being guided to her berth on the North River. (Planet News)

Perhaps because of that broadcast, all who sailed in Maurie on that homeward run were very much on the alert. Passengers later revealed that her captain never left the bridge and had even made his bed there. The liner had zig-zagged all the way across the Atlantic, but except for intensive life-boat drill, the routine was normal.

News — given out so glibly abroad, even by America, before December 7, 1941 — sometimes made nonsense of the strict censorship prevailing in Britain. In March, 1940, for example, New York was telling the world, particularly the Axis, that Britain's Queen Mary and the Mauretania were to be pressed into service as troopships for the transportation of Australian soldiers to war zones.

"The disclosure," to quote an Associated Press report at that time, "came with the arrival here of the Cunard White Star liner Antonia, which carried 700 officers and men as a complement to the skeleton crews of the two other Cunard White Star vessels lying here. Secrecy (!) surrounded the Antonia's arrival, and all visitors were barred from the pier. Cunard White Star officials declined to comment on the projected transfer of the seamen. United States Custom officials said they did not inspect the luggage of the British seamen because they were informed that the men would be transferred tomorrow to the other liners."

A rare shot of the Mauretania as a troopship steaming through the Panama Canal early in 1940. (Wide World Photos)

A subsequent A.P. report informed how "the crack liner Queen Mary was getting up steam at midnight (New York time) last night, four hours after the Mauretania had sailed out of New York Harbour . . . .

"It was believed that the Queen Mary would join the Mauretania on the high seas and that the two liners would then head for Australia, via Cape Horn. Seamen believe that both ships will first call at Halifax, Nova Scotia, to be defensively armed for the voyage."

Another report stated that by removing the Queen Mary's peacetime furnishings, normal passenger capacity of about 2,000 had been increased to 21,000, and supplies sufficient for three to four months had been taken on board.

Whether or not German agents on and around New York's waterfront would have revealed all, anyway, is beside the point. The captains of those two great liners must have been in a muck sweat with anticipation of the enemy's reaction when they put to sea after these reports.

Adding to this mockery of secrecy were further reports of the Mauretania's progress — from her lying in Cristobal Bay, to her sailing through the Panama Canal to Balboa, where she refuelled; leaving the latter "for an undisclosed destination", with hints at Australia — and even being sighted off Honolulu.

Happily, both these magnificent liners survived the war and in February, 1946, it was revealed by the Bethlehem Steel Corporation that the big four Cunarders, Queen Elizabeth, Queen Mary, Aquitania and Mauretania, had been armed and converted in New York Harbour. The QM was fitted with 33 guns, 12 rocket-projectiles, a range-finder, a central gun-house and degaussing apparatus.

Splendid old Aquitania, which would probably have been retired about the beginning of the war, helped keep the passenger traffic flowing between Britain and America while the Queens and Maurie were at war. She was not finally withdrawn from service until the end of 1949, having crossed the Atlantic between the wars nearly 600 times and carrying $1\frac{1}{4}$ million passengers. She was 35 years old.

Still a troopship, Mauretania again became "public property" when she glided into the Mersey in May 1945.

Few of the well-informed Merseyside river-front workers and regular ferry passengers failed to recognise her once-familiar lines, in spite of her drab paint. She had steamed more than half a million miles on wartime duties.

Mauretania returning to Liverpool with 4,000 troops in September, 1945, shortly after the last war. (D.P. & E.)

Her first "official" post-war visit to Liverpool to land thousands of service personnel, came on September 24, 1945, after a 24-hour delay because of bad weather. Captain R.B.G. Woollatt reported that the liner had broken some records. She had completed virtually a round-the-world voyage of 28,662 sea miles in 81 days, 16 hours — a record for passenger vessels of her type. She had also sailed from Sydney to the Mersey Bar in a month and a day — 13,700 miles. Allowing for time in port, she had averaged 21 knots.

This round-the-world record was quickly challenged by the Royal Mail Lines, which claimed that its liner, the Andes (26,000 tons), which had left Liverpool on June 29, had made the voyage in 72 days, 8 hours, 55 minutes. Her steaming distance was 26,012 and her average daily steaming distance was 361.3 miles, compared with Mauretania's 349.5.

Cunard hit back. Mauretania's ocean steaming time was 56 days, 6 hours, 32 minutes, they said. Mauretania's average daily steaming distance was 509.28 miles.

So, it was a doubly-proud Maurie 2 which sailed for the Far East from the Mersey on October 21, 1945, her funnels newly painted in the Cunard colours once more.

But the following day, the liner Orion, berthing at Southampton, claimed the round-the-world record as hers. Her commander, Captain A.C.G. Hawker said: "We have also gone round the world through the Panama Canal to New Zealand and Sydney and back by way of Bombay and the Suez Canal, in 74 days . . . We also beat the Mauretania's record of one month and one day from Britain to Sydney."

Nothing like a bit of friendly rivalry to keep the great liners moving, it seemed!

When the large-scale movements to Canada of 29,454 wives and 10,139 children of Canadian servicemen overseas began in February, 1946, Mauretania made the first trip from Liverpool to Halifax on February 5 with the largest contingent. She carried 400 wives and two of her public rooms were converted into nurseries for their 364 babies, 64 of whom were under a year old.

Meanwhile, hundreds of brides from abroad were also coming into Britain to make new homes with their ex-service husbands. Within two hours of Maurie's leaving Liverpool, the Cunarder Samaria arrived at Liverpool with 800 brides and children from South Africa. Many anxious husbands were waiting to greet them, in some cases eager to see their children who had been born after they had set out for England and demobilisation.

Seventeen-months-old Yvonne Buxton, the daughter of Corporal R.H. Buxton, of Manchester, arrived with a gold sovereign clutched in her tiny hand. Although she didn't know it, she was fulfilling a family tradition which the South African leader, General Smuts himself, had helped perpetuate. When Yvonne's grandparents had heard of her impending birth, they wanted to maintain the tradition that every new-born member of the family should have a golden sovereign placed in its hand at birth. Export bullion was prohibited then, and the family appealed to General Smuts, who carried the coin from London to the Cape and forwarded it to Yvonne's father, who was still serving there.

Another passenger in the Samaria that day who had gold in mind, was the Comptesse de Serret, who had come to Britain to collect valuables smuggled from France to England at the time of the German occupation.

For the wide-eyed kids who had spent their lives in toy-starved Britain, the huge selection of toys awaiting them on the Mauretania on February 5 must have seemed like a grand grotto and Christmas all over again. In charge of the catering for the mothers and children was Chief Steward George Baker, for whom the experience must have been a memorable one. George had been personally responsible for the comfort of Winston Churchill on all that great war leader's trans-Atlantic crossings.

Mauretania's homeward voyage to Liverpool was in complete contrast to that first leg. She returned with 2,753 German prisoners of war, who were to work on British farms in place of repatriated Italian prisoners. In fact, Mauretania took nearly 5,000 Italian prisoners of war to Toronto from Liverpool on June 2. Members of the crew compared the return voyage to Liverpool as funereal with the party atmosphere which had prevailed on the outward passage. The prisoners, mostly ex-Africa Corps, were confined in the liners third class accommodation behind barbed-wire barriers, but gave no trouble.

More brides and more prisoners were to be Maurie's lot for some time, although in May she had the pleasant task of bringing to Liverpool more than 800 members of the Indian and Burmese forces, who took part in the Victory Parade in London on June 8th. Among them were three VC's and the Maharajah of Dewas, on his first visit to England. He acted as senior ADC to the King at the ceremony.

In August, 1946, the liner made a record-breaking return passage from Liverpool to Singapore, taking 15 days, 20 hours, 31 minutes for the outward run, and 16 days, 1 hour, 50 minutes for the homeward run.

After some $6\frac{1}{2}$ years of splendid trooping service, Maurie made her last voyage as a transport on August 19, 1946, when, fittingly, she carried Field Marshal Viscount Montgomery to Canada for a visit at the invitation of the Canadian Government. Two other famous passengers were the Archbishop of Canterbury, Dr. Geoffrey Fisher, and Mrs. Fisher and Chief Scout, Lord Rowallan, for whom a guard of honour, composed of 500 Boy Scouts, formed on Liverpool's landing stage.

Back home in Liverpool, in Gladstone Dock, and in the skilled hands of 1,500 men from Cammell Laird's, her birthplace, Maurie underwent a six-month conversion to transform her once more into the luxurious liner she was meant to be before the war had so rudely interrupted the life of glamour for which she had really been created. Among the tons of wartime paraphernalia disgorged by the ship at this time, including beds, hammocks, linen, mattresses, troop-tables and crockery, was a heap of tiny paper-mache baths — used by all those infants she had carried as one of the world's largest floating nurseries!

Maurie's return to normal commercial service signalled a big reshuffle in Cunard's passenger liner operations. Liverpool lost Maurie, not to London again, but to Southampton, and the reconditioned 26,000-ton Britannic and two new 14,000-tonners in the Media and the Parthia, came to Liverpool. Veterans Franconia, Samaria and Scythia maintained the Liverpool-Halifax service, the Ascania running to Quebec and Montreal. Maurie went south to assist the two giant Queens and the scheduled 30,000-ton Caronia — the new fleet intended for the fast Southampton-Le Havre-New York service to capture the continental traffic.

This, however, did not take place immediately and, on April 19, 1947, under the command of Captain Woollatt, Maurie left Liverpool for her "shake-down" trials, with many Merseyside V.I.P.'s among her 400 passengers. Cunard's tradition of all-male pursers was broken on this occasion when two ex-WRNS, Mrs. Phylis Davies, of Bristol, and Miss Margaret Morton, of Glasgow, sailed as assistant pursers.

In spite of violent gales, which kept the liner at the Mersey Bar for three days, and upsetting quite a few mayoral and businessmen's engagements, "she behaved like a lady under every test made," said Captain Woollatt. The Liverpool Daily Post and Echo sent regular bulletins to the news-starved passengers and crew during this long delay . . . so close to home.

After a turn-round conducted at breakneck speed, Maurie kept her appointment for her first commercial, post-war voyage. Refurbished, revictualled and shipshape, she left Liverpool on April 26. New York gave her another rousing welcome when she berthed there on May 3, having covered the 3,192 miles from Liverpool to Ambrose Light in 6 days, 2 minutes, averaging 22.16 knots. She made the return trip to Liverpool at an average speed of 24.33 knots.

An experiment of placing two Customs men on the ship to speed customs clearance was made for the first time on this route and on this maiden voyage. It proved a great success.

Among her outward passengers were the Hollywood star, Sabu ("the Elephant Boy"); Sir (then Mr.) John Moores, founder of the Littlewoods Organisation (pools, mail-order and chain stores), and his wife, Mrs. Ruby Moores; Sir Arthur Sutherland, the Tyneside shipowner, and the British legless wartime air-ace, Group Captain Douglas Bader.

On May 21, Maurie said goodbye to the Mersey for a time when she left Liverpool for New York with a full passenger list, returning to her new base at Southampton on her homeward voyage. For many years she went winter cruising and became a leading "dollar-earner". During four sunshine cruises from New York to the West Indies, in 1950, she earned nearly three million dollars in passenger fares and about 86,000 dollars in sales from the ship's bars, shops and show cases.

A bit of a fuss was caused in August, 1948, when Maurie was compelled to wait in a gale outside Cobh, where she had called to pick up 250 passengers on passage for Canada. People were amazed that she did not enter the harbour, particularly when the United States liner, Washington, steamed past her to enter the inner harbour. Captain Barnes, the harbour master, said there would have

This picturesque little pleasure steamer was originally the "Queen" of Southampton. She was renamed "Mauretania" to oblige the Cunard Line and later became the "Corfe Castle". (See page 97).

111

been no trouble in swinging her in on the flood tide, but Cunard reckoned that the company's experts considered Maurie too big to enter Cobh and that no risk could be taken.

One of the worst storms that seaworthy ship encountered arose in November, 1952, when she battled through a hurricane on her passage to New York. Her master, then Captain Donald Sorrell, said that 47 passengers had been treated for minor bruises and there were three cases of damaged ribs and one scalp wound. A cross-sea smashed windows as high as her enclosed promenade-deck and even entered her main-deck square. Jesse Royce Landis, the American stage and film actress, said she was thrown from one end of the saloon to the other, with chairs piling on top of her. Many passengers sat up all of one night, wearing their life-jackets.

Passengers in the French liner, Liberte, making the crossing at the same time, also suffered some injuries. Captain Jacques Lefevre said that some of the waves broke over the ship's funnels — 120 feet above the waterline.

But one passenger didn't mind that rough weather a bit. He was "Mr.Ramshaw", the golden-eagle pet of Kent naturalist Captain C.W.R.Knight, making his 27th Atlantic crossing with his master. "He's used to sitting around on top of trees in the Scottish Highlands and being blown all over the place," said Captain Knight.

Mauretania steamed into Liverpool from New York again in December, 1953, for overhaul after a long absence. She landed nearly 500 passengers — the first civil passengers she had ever carried to Liverpool. For her crew of 593, it meant a long Christmas holiday on Merseyside, where most of them belonged.

Her visit to Liverpool called for a celebration and, the day before she left, on January 16, 1954, four of her former masters lunched on board with the current master, Captain A.B. Fasting. The quartet were: Captain C. Ivan Thompson, of Grassendale, Liverpool, then Captain of the Queen Elizabeth and Commodore of the Cunard fleet, who had joined the company in 1916 and had served in practically all of their liners and through two world wars without mishap; Captain G.E. Cove, former Commodore of the fleet, of West Derby, Liverpool, who retired in October, 1952; Captain R.B.G. Woollatt, of Greasby, Wirral, Mauretania's commander when she made her record-breaking troopship voyage from the Far East to Liverpool in 1945, and Captain Harry Dixon, of Wallasey, Merseyside, who had retired in May, 1951.

Such men were not just uniform and gold braid, as the passengers on the Mauretania found out on their way to Liverpool from New York in June, 1956, when the liner called at Cobh. The tender, Killarney, which had been serving the liner, backed off and fouled her propeller with a six-inch rope. Hearing of her plight, Maurie's Staff Captain P.A. Reade, RNR, a keen sub-aqua sportsman, donned his wet suit and eventually cleared the entangled prop with a butcher's knife after 25 minutes work. Passengers lining the Mauretania's deck rails loudly cheered his expertise.

Although Mauretania's visits to her Liverpool birthplace were relatively few, she was always warmly welcomed. An example of this is contained in the columns of the Liverpool Daily Post of October 2, 1957.

"It always delights me to discover how many of the people who live along the banks of the Mersey swear undying allegiance to the great liners which frequent the river. Yet among the ship-fanciers there are an unhappy few who have lost their hearts to a girl who frequents another port — that lovely daughter of Merseyside, the Mauretania. For me, and a good many others, autumn turns back to summer tomorrow, when our lady returns to our midst for her winter overhaul. I cannot believe that any Merseysider who lived through the war years here can be quite unmoved by this particular Cunarder's return to Liverpool. Of all the ships which battled purposefully across the submarine-infested Atlantic, carrying fighting men and war material, the Mauretania had a habit of slipping into the mouth of her native river, unshaken and punctual to the hour, with the regularity of a ferry-boat."

Those were the days when winter overhauls for the big liners meant work for the men of Merseyside, and six more Cunarders which followed Maurie into the docks for overhaul that winter were the Britannic, Carinthia, Ivernia, Sylvania, Media and Parthia. Nineteen-years-old Maurie was air-conditioned throughout during her 15 weeks at Liverpool. On her 1962 overhaul, this time at Southampton, the liner's familiar black and white livery was replaced by her new colours of cruising green, previously worn only by the Caronia.

Mr. John Partington, of Hooton, Wirral, a former seagoing printer with Cunard, recalled that "when seen from a distance at sea, the Maurie could easily be mistaken for the Queen Elizabeth.

"This changed when she was painted in green cruising colours and some sailors distastefully dubbed her the 'Gangrene Queen,' " he said.

Merseyside did not see Maurie again until 1963 when, she returned from a series of cruises, based on Naples. Passengers and relief crew were flown out from the U.K. on charter flights to join her there. Cunard had hoped to pick up some of the Italian and European business, but the experiment was not very successful.

Whispers of Maurie's reaching the end of her useful life began in June, 1965, but Cunard did not confirm this until October, when the company announced that she was to be sold for scrap on her return

her there. Cunard had hoped to pick up some of the Italian and southern European business, but the experiment was not very successful.

Completely unrecognisable as the once-proud, world-renowned luxury liner, Mauretania (II), now a hulk, lies on the mud flats of the breakers' yard at Inverkeithing. (Photocraft)

from a Mediterranean cruise. She was sold to Thomas W. Ward and Company, of Inverkeithing, Scotland, for an undisclosed sum.

Maurie was the largest complete ship ever to be broken up at Inverkeithing — in the same yard which had dispatched such illustrious ships as the British warships Howe, Rodney and Revenge, in addition to many more Cunard and White Star liners.

So, Maurie returned to Southampton on November 10, 1965, without so much as a whistle of respect for her presence. Several hundred Americans, who had then ended the 56-day cruise, transferred to the Queen Mary to return to New York. A wee poodle, named Adonne, owned by Mrs. Billie Helsing, of Cherry Chase, Maryland, came with her. And just to prove that quarantine regulations were upheld, Adonne had to be carried in a wicker basket from one ship to the other, without his feet touching the ground!

An interesting sidelight on Maurie's wartime career is that her magnificent furniture was lent to Liverpool and used to equip a number of mansions taken over to accommodate refugees and repatriates passing through Merseyside. As a result, many hostels were given a distinct atmosphere of luxury. The return of this expensive furniture to Cunard, when the Mauretania was refitting for commerce again, was extremely helpful in speeding her refitting at a time when "utility" furniture was all that could be had on the post-war market.

Newfoundland (I) and (II) & Nova Scotia (I) and (II)

Right from the start, Warren Line's 6,791-ton liner, Newfoundland, on the company's North Atlantic service, seemed destined to be a "rescue ship". And at least five incidents gave credence to this epithet.

Built by Vickers Armstrong, of Barrow, in 1925, she had a disruptive maiden voyage from Liverpool to St.John's, Halifax and Boston, on June 16 that year,when she had to put into Belfast with a piston defect. She was then carrying a shipwrecked crew who were being returned to St.John, Nova Scotia. Their vessel, the Florence Swythens, had foundered in the Atlantic and they had been landed at Alicante.

Less than four months later, on October 6, the Newfoundland had brought to Liverpool a captain and his crew who had earlier survived a perilous voyage in a small vessel. They had left Middlesborough on August 26 in the Coalopolis, a tug of only 175 tons and 95 feet long, bound for Halifax, Nova Scotia. The weather throughout the voyage was foul and she had to put into Loch Ariboll. After moving on to Stornaway for bunkering, the tug thrust out into the wild Atlantic for St. John's, Newfoundland. Heavy seas swept Coalopolis from stem to stern and the crew, their accommodation awash, had to eat and sleep above the boilers to protect themselves from the sea.

On arrival at St.John's, the tug had only 14 tons of coal left, but, rebunkered, she bravely went back into the storm and finally made Halifax, her destination.

Newfoundland arrived at Liverpool on October 22, 1935, with 21 of the crew of the 100-ton Danish fishing schooner, Coronet, which had been badly damaged in a storm. A gale had carried away the main mast and lifeboat and it took them 13 days, with a jury-rigged sail, to battle back into a port near St.John's.

Incident No.3 was a "rescue that wasn't . . . . " The story arose from a claim for salvage remuneration by Newfoundland's owners in the Admiralty Court in November, 1935, against the London owners of the steamer, Tower Bridge.

In the thick of North Atlantic pack-ice, Newfoundland had gone to the rescue of the Tower Bridge in response to the latter's S.O.S. The steamer's owners contended that the liner was never seen and that, when the wireless advice from the Newfoundland, to turn about and go east, was given, the Tower Bridge was already diverting south and east.

President Sir Boyd Merriman said that the Tower Bridge, holed and taking in water, was taken out of danger by the Newfoundland

Newfoundland (I), known as the "rescue ship" for her brave exploits. She served with distinction as a hospital ship in the last war. (Furness Withy Group)

(which she never saw) by following her into safety by means only of her wireless connection. Captain Weller of the Newfoundland had accepted a great responsibility in taking his ship through the pack-ice, said the president. He had damaged a propeller but never hesitated to respond to the S.O.S. His Lordship made a £2,000 award — £1,500 to the Newfoundland's owners, £200 to her master and £300 to the crew.

Again, in March, 1939, it was Newfoundland to the rescue. This time, she answered an S.O.S. from a disabled and sinking sealing ship, the Ranger, in a gale off Newfoundland. After many hours of considerable difficulties in appalling conditions, with rough seas in a temperature seven degrees below freezing, the liner succeeded in taking off 18 of the sealer's crew. Another vessel, the sealing ship Imogene, finally towed the Ranger to safety. Newfoundland's master, Captain James Walter Murphy, Chief Officer Rowland F. Handley, in charge of the lifeboat, and other members of the liner's crew involved in this brave rescue, later received awards from the Liverpool Shipwreck and Humane Society, presented by the Lord Mayor of Liverpool, Alderman Sir Sidney Jones.

Requisitioned as a hospital ship in September, 1940, the Newfoundland served with distinction during the war. After service as a base hospital ship at Bathurst, West Africa, she made a number of voyages from Britain to Canada with wounded and sick Canadian troops. She suffered damage when striking a mine off Casablanca and also some minor damage in air raids at Algiers and Philippeville. Then, on September 13, 1943, serving in the North Africa campaign, she was bombed and later sunk off Agropoli. Five British Red Cross nurses, all the doctors, the junior engineer and five of the 106 crew were among the 23 killed. Survivors told how the Newfoundland had carried all her lights and huge red crosses in compliance with the Geneva Convention.

In his report to the C-in-C, Mediterranean, her master, Captain J.E. Wilson, told how, while anchored off Agropoli about 11 a.m. on Sunday, September 12, an aircraft dropped a large bomb, which fell between the Newfoundland and the Saint Andrew, another hospital ship. No damage was sustained and the ships were ordered to another anchorage much further away. The Leinster, also a hospital ship, was at this anchorage, too, and about 6.15 p.m. another enemy dive-bombing attack was made on all three "protected" ships. No damage was sustained and they all moved out to sea.

"This was a deliberate attack on three hospital ships in daylight . . ." said Captain Wilson. He went on to explain that, the following day, when Newfoundland, Saint Andrew, Leinster and the Amapoora were standing off, awaiting the time of re-entry to the beaches, "a further absolutely deliberate dive-bombing attack was made at 0510 hours. All ships were fully illuminated at the time, according to the Geneva Convention ruling. The Newfoundland was set on fire almost immediately and owing to several small boats being shattered and/or set on fire, the remaining boats were in the process of being lowered when the boats from the Leinster and Saint Andrew arrived and disembarkation proceeded." Their passengers were taken to Bizerta.

The chief casualties were confined to the hospital staff who had been sleeping on the open deck because of the warm night. Although five British nurses were killed, 103 American nurses, waiting to land with the Fifth Army, survived. But there was no rescue for gallant Newfoundland in her dire distress.

At 0610, a big explosion occured in the vicinity of the bomb crater, which led the Captain to think that the oil-fuel tank, deep amidships, had caught fire. He ordered all the crew away but for 17 officers and men in the hope that they might still save the ship. But all the fire-fighting equipment had been rendered useless by the bombing.

Two American destroyers and a salvage tug eventually came to the liner's aid and by midnight the fire was quelled. A start was then made to pump out the considerable amount of water in the stricken ship (it was 12 feet deep in the engine-room), which had given her a 15 degree list. Two small holes were also burned in her side to help the drainage and the salvage vessel was made fast for towing.

"However," reported Captain Wilson, "the authorities decided that, in view of the position ashore, the tug could not be spared and the vessel was sunk by gunfire, approximately 70 shells being fired at her."

Nova Scotia (I), honoured with a silk flag of Nova Scotia for her long association with the Province.

Naturally, Captain Wilson was not at all pleased with this order, believing that Newfoundland, which was also carrying valuable stores, could have been saved and eventually rendered serviceable again. "... I protest strongly at the sinking of this vessel," he wrote.

Captain Wilson was awarded the O.B.E. and his second officer, the B.E.M. Four members of the crew were mentioned in the London Gazette.

Said the oldest survivor, 60-year-old crew member, Mr. Tom Rowlands, of Liverpool, "It was the most criminal attack I have ever experienced." And Tom would have known. He had been shipwrecked four times before that in his 45 years at sea.

Newfoundland's sister-ship, the 6,796-ton Nova Scotia, first of her name to be built for the Furness Line service, made her maiden voyage from Liverpool to Boston in May, 1926. Although she made some winter cruises from New York to the West Indies in 1927 and 1928, she was chiefly employed in the Liverpool-Halifax-Boston service. The Province of Nova Scotia had honoured her association with it by presenting the liner with a silk flag of the Province. This was hung in her entrance hall. She and the Newfoundland continued in their North Atlantic service for the first year of the war until requisitioned by the Government in 1940.

Fitted out as a troopship in 1941, Nova Scotia carried more than a thousand troops to Suez, via the Cape, and subsequently was employed carrying South African troops to Egypt and returning with Italian prisoners of war from Egypt. While on passage with some of

Newfoundland (II), above, leaving the Mersey for the last time. She followed her sister, Nova Scotia (II), below, to Glasgow for extensive alterations before starting on the Australia-Japan route for the Dominion Navigation Company, of Nassau. (Top picture, D.P. & E.: lower picture, Furness Withy Group)

the latter on December 4, 1942, she was torpedoed by a U.boat near Laurenco Marques, only a day's run from Durban. Two torpedoes sank her in about seven minutes.

A Portuguese sloop picked up the survivors, but from her crew of 117 only 18 were saved. The majority of the large number of Italian evacuees from Eritrea, including the occupants of Asmara Gaol and the escort, were also lost.

Replacements for both these ships after the war operated from Liverpool to Boston under the Furness-Warren Line. Nova Scotia, a 7,438-ton liner, carrying 75 first-class and 80 tourist-class passengers, built in 1947, made her maiden voyage on September 2 that year. Like her predecessor, she was also honoured with a silk flag from the Province.

Newfoundland, with the same tonnage and passenger capacity, and built the following year, made her maiden voyage on February 14, 1948. Her last scheduled voyage for Furness Withy was in a mercy dash across the Atlantic to Cork to land a 17-year-old crew member, seriously ill with acute appendicitis. That was in October, 1962, when the company was inviting offers for both Newfoundland and Nova Scotia because of the falling passenger trade.

Both ships were sold to the Dominion Navigation Company, of Nassau, for service on the Australia-Japan route. Nova Scotia left the Mersey for the last time on November 12, 1962. Nova Scotia, renamed Francis Drake, and the Newfoundland, renamed George Anson, were both broken up in 1971-72.

The company's links with Nova Scotia were brought to mind again on Merseyside in April, 1965, when a former master, Captain J.E. Wilson, who had retired after 40 years service at sea, presented a Nova Scotian flag to Captain John H. Williams, master of the cargo vessel, Nova Scotia, shortly before her maiden voyage.

Seven weeks of exploring uninhabited and uncharted parts of Newfoundland lie before these excited young men, pictured ready to sail on the liner Novia Scotia in September, 1947. (D.P. & E.)

Orduña

All ships have histories, of course, but some just happen to have had more flamboyant careers than others. Apart from the giants of maritime history, like the Titanic (which wrote herself into posterity without so much as completing her maiden voyage), a large number of vessels are chiefly remembered for their war exploits.

The 15,499-ton Orduña — nicknamed "Will o' the Wisp o' the Ocean" — was such a ship. Built by Harland & Wolff at Belfast she was launched on October 2, and made her maiden voyage from Liverpool to Valparaiso on February 19, 1914. She made doubly sure of earning her niche in the archives of famous vessels with some notable wartime experiences. This was the ship whose wily master fooled Germany in the Great War by improvising dummy guns from ventilators, and which later sank a U. boat with real guns. Orduña belonged to the Pacific Steam Navigation Company, to whom Merseyside owes a great deal.

This is the oldest operating shipping company in the port, whose once huge trading fleet, affectionately known as "The Birkenhead Navy," included the beautiful passenger-liner "Queens" — the Reina del Pacifico and the Reina del Mar. Some of Britain's firmest trade links with South America have been forged by P.S.N.C. ships, which have sailed from the Mersey ever since American William Wheelwright founded the line in 1838. Many are the wonderful stories of these ships, whose ultra-modern sisters, still operating

"Will o' the Wisp" Orduna, dressed overall.
(Pacific Steam Navigation Company Ltd.)

121

prosperously today, helped bestow on their company the honour of the Queens Award for Exports in 1978, and whose names, for almost one and a half centuries, have included the prefix "Or" — Latin for gold, with which ancient South America always will be associated.

Ships with names like Orbita, Orcades, Oropesa, Orotava, Orissa and Ortega, during the company's long history have been involved in some amazing exploits, especially during the various wars, some now half-forgotten by most of the world, like those between Peru and Chile and the American Civil War. Right at the outset of the young company, the P.S.N.C. flag in the 1840's saw hostile action, when its original vessels, the Chile and the Peru, were armed with two small two-pounder cannon against pirates.

Orduna was built in the grim year of 1914 as a passenger liner and the company's first triple-screw vessel, for the usual service to the east and west coasts of South America. She made her maiden voyage from Liverpool to South America on February 19th, that year. She could have been the first ship to sail through the brand-new Panama Canal, which links the Atlantic with the Pacific, but, with true British "noblesse oblige," she held back for an American ship to take this honour. The liner was on only her second voyage when World War 1 broke out. She was anchored at Balboa, Panama and, homeward-bound, had the opportunity to achieve another "first" by being the largest liner to pass through the Canal. But a landslide there put paid to this. She was faced with the prospect of sailing the long way round through the Straits of Magellan, at a time when prowling German battle cruisers were looking for victims such as she.

The company's Coast Manager informed Orduna's veteran master, Captain Tom McComb Taylor, of Wallasey, that because of this threat, something should be done to make the liner appear to be armed. A "brainstorming" session was held, which resulted in a memorable ruse ; . . . .

Two long deck ventilation tubes, of the type used for ventilating the holds, were unshipped, and, with the addition of some packing cases and canvas, all cunningly painted, Orduna was mounted with a couple of deadly-looking guns! As Captain Taylor was a RNR man, he was entitled to use the naval blue flags. So, the Admiralty "Jack" flew convincingly above the dummies.

A trader, Orduna still had business in other ports as she sailed south. And her "guns" were quickly spotted. At Callao, the Captain of the Port demanded that the liner's guns be dismantled immediately as Orduna was in a neutral port and the Germans had lodged an objection.

He was invited on board, where he and his entourage, including some port officials, were taken to see the "guns". And when the covers were withdrawn, their faces were a study! Looks of amazement turned to grins, chuckles, and then hearty laughter. The party adjourned to split a bottle of champagne and to toast the armed-merchantman-that-never-was. The dummies were dismantled until Orduna sailed and she continued her voyage to find that her fame had gone ahead of her at the various ports of call.

At this stage of the war, an act like arming a merchant ship without officially listing her as such simply was not "cricket," and the Germans were blazing. Orduna reached Valparaiso to find the German Consul raging, but when Admiral Gomez Carreno, representing the Chilean Government, came on board to see the guns, he roared with laughter, too. The scene of merriment was like that at Callao. But Orduna was ordered, by cable, to dismantle the dummies before leaving Valparaiso.

On her way home, and having reached the eastern seaboard of South America, Orduna was signalled by HMS Glasgow which asked if she could spare any RNR men on board. About ten men responded — and a Conway boy cadet. The latter did well at the original Battle of the Falkland Islands, coolly fetching water for the guns and rolling cigarettes for the gunners!

Back home at Liverpool, graceful Orduna, her luxurious and ornate rooms still virtually unseasoned by the tobacco of that heavy-smoking age, was needed on the North Atlantic. She was chartered to Cunard, and with her went Captain Taylor and her PSNC officers and engineers. As a wartime passenger liner and, later, an armed merchantman, her speed, manoeuverability and capacity for getting out of trouble fast, resulted in her being tagged 'Will o' the Wisp' and "The Elusive Liner". She certainly bore a charmed life.

At 3.30 p.m. on July 8, 1915, Orduna left Liverpool with 227 passengers, half of whom were women and children. Twenty-two were Americans. The following morning, a few minutes after six, when some 35 miles south of Queenstown (Cobh), the wake of a U. boat's torpedo could be seen tracing its way to the ship. The missile passed the liner's stern by no more than ten feet.

When the submarine surfaced and fired seven shells at the now-fleeing liner, the latter was a mile and a half away. Orduna carried no ammunition. The U. boat gave up the chase. It simply could not match the speed of Will o' the Wisp, or the seamanship of her commander, who dutifully remained on the bridge in that perilous U. boat zone for some 26 hours without a break. There had been no panic. Passengers wore their life-jackets and some were observed to be carrying their jewellery and other treasured possessions, too. They kept under cover until the "all-clear".

The following day, the passengers who included the Baron and Baroness Rosenkrantz, passed a resolution of thanks and admiration to Captain Taylor, saying that it was entirely due to his skill,

Top: R.M.S. Ortega (1906). Below: The Orissa (1898).
(Pictures: Pacific Steam Navigation Company Ltd.)

resourcefulness and unfailing pluck that they had escaped. The first ship to congratulate Captain Taylor on this encounter was the Isle of Man steamer, Snaefell, doing her wartime duty as a naval patrol ship (later sunk by a U.boat in the Mediterranean), and whose commander, coincidentally, was another PSNC master, Captain Green.

Orduna became almost shipping target No. 1 for the frustrated Germans, who made every effort to sink her. In November, 1916, in a special operation, they sent a U. boat, with a picked crew of 90, under strict orders to finish her off. Instead of netting Will o' the Wisp, they suffered the ignominy of being caught themselves — in the steel mesh of a British anti-submarine net — and captured alive.

Captain Taylor, son of a Peterhead bookseller, was one of the greatest seamen of his day. Taylor, his Chief Engineer, Tom Gowans, and Orduna made a formidable trio and continued to sight and elude enemy submarines throughout the war. But, like all good seadogs, they did have their day . . . .

This was early in June, 1918, when Orduna's lookout spotted a U. boat as the liner was ploughing through a blanket of mist. The foggy shape at first was thought to be a fishing boat, but then the conning tower and two periscopes were seen.

"Run her down!" shouted Captain Taylor. But Orduna was a split second too late. She missed ramming the U. boat by a mere six feet. So close did she come to crushing the submarine that, as this swept by alongside, a few of the liner's off-duty firemen threw clinkers at some of the German crew on deck.

Then Orduna, now armed with some very real guns, brought these to bear on the U. boat, partly submerged, abreast of amidships and only about 70 feet away. A few seconds later, a shell from the liner's stern gun struck the base of the sub's conning tower and down she went in an explosion of smoke and flame.

Captain Taylor and Chief Gowans each received the O.B.E. for their splendid war record — presented by the King, with his personal congratulations, that same month. A fine gift of silver candelabra was also given to Captain Taylor by the Cunard Company, with whom the liner was then serving. Nor did Taylor's invaluable service end there. Like Captain Sam Robinson (in command of the Empress of Australia at the Yokohama earthquake in 1923) Captain Taylor, as master of the Orissa, lowered his boats and filled his ship with refugees from an earthquake which hit Valparaiso.

On another occasion, when the Russian barque, Lord Torridan, was dismasted and sinking in the wintry mid-Atlantic Captain Taylor found that, because of the high seas, the masters of two steamers would not take the risk of trying to assist. But Taylor did

Orduna tied up at Prince's Landing Stage, Liverpool, in January, 1951, after making her last voyage from Singapore. Aged 37, she was then due for scrapping. (Observer Photos)

not hesitate. He lowered his boats and rescued every man Jack, including the master's pet dog.

A mariner of the old school, Captain Taylor had a nerve of steel but always effaced himself to give credit to others. He was also a keen golfer, who even played occasionally when at sea! To prevent balls flying off the deck, he invented a special ball with a tiny parachute attached . . . probably not even imagining that in an era yet to come, fast-landing aircraft would have similar attachments!

Reconverted in 1919 for peacetime duties, Orduna was chartered to the Royal Mail Steam Packet Company until 1927, when she returned to her original service runs between Liverpool and South America.

In August, 1938, Lord Baden-Powell, the Chief Scout, with Lady Baden-Powell, the Chief Guide, and some 440 Scouts and Guides from many countries, sailed from Liverpool in the Orduna on a "peace-fostering cruise," to Iceland, Norway, Denmark and Belgium. This 17-day voyage was the third similar cruise, the first being in 1933, and the second, the year after. They called at one port in each country, where they were welcomed by Scouts and Guides. Lord Baden-Powell, then 82, did not go ashore, but clad in uniform, welcomed his guests on board and addressed them there.

A nice little yarn concerning Orduna (when Captain Arthur George Litherland was in command) was published in *"The Steam Conquistadores,"* by John Lingwood, P.S.N.C.'s archivist, in *"Sea Breezes"* magazine of April, 1977. This referred to the liner's leaving Freetown during the last war, when her speed was too high for the rest of the convoy she was in . . . .

"Consequently, she kept going ahead and stopping, until the convoy caught up. A frustrated destroyer-escort captain came up and signalled: 'If you want to play races, I've got 27 knots on my side.' Unfortunately, in his approach, he bumped the Orduna, whose quick reply was: 'If you want to play races, I've got 15,000 tons on my side!' "

Requisitioned as a troopship in 1941, Orduna never returned to her old role and, in December, 1946, under Captain J. Williams, she carried 2,400 Moslem pilgrims from Jeddah to Beirut.

"The strangest voyage of my career," Captain Williams wrote in the August, 1949, issue of 'Sea Breezes'. "To get any order amongst the pilgrims was almost an impossibility; for, once on deck with their bundles and packs, neither water-hoses nor sticks could shift them," he said. "You can drive sheep and cattle, but it was entirely useless to try and reason with these people.

". . . . We sailed from Jeddah on December 10 and called en route at El Tor, in the Gulf of Suez, which is an Egyptian quarantine station. Here, all our passengers were taken ashore to pass through a turnstile to be checked, and then through a disinfectant chamber, where they were sprayed and deloused. Twelve failed to report as they had booked their passage to Paradise via 'Davy Jones's Locker;' they had died on passage . . . ."

Orduna continued in government service and carried troops and civil service personnel to the Far East until 1951, when she was broken up. Her old master, Captain Taylor, however, had long before said farewell to her, when among those who watched her depart from Liverpool in August, 1939, and sail away into World War II. "It was like meeting an old friend and losing her again," said the gallant seaman, whose name forever will be one with this ship.

Reina del Pacifico

Described on her trials as a "wonder ship", and the largest and most powerful British motorship at that time, the Reina del Pacifico was a true "queen" on any ocean. This four-screw, 20-knot, 17,800-ton Pacific Steam Navigation Company's vessel, built and engined by Harland and Wolff, Belfast, operated on the Liverpool-West Coast of South America service for 27 years and became one of the best-known Liverpool liners. Building her in 1931 was said to have been "an act of faith", and she didn't let the company down.

A three-class liner, with an all-white hull and green boot-topping, she was the largest ship in the fleet and in naming her, the company broke away from the traditional "O"-classification, with which so many of their passenger ships were prefixed. Her public rooms were designed, decorated and furnished in the Mooresque and Colonial periods — a theme appreciated by those who used this service, which linked Europe (with calls at ports in Spain) and the Latin-American continent. She had a magnificent grand hall, the height of two decks and a winter garden modelled on a courtyard of old Spain. Captain Ellis Roberts, her master on the occasion of her shakedown cruise, declared that she was "the finest ship I have ever stepped on board".

The trials of this famous ship created a little piece of Irish history in that the standard of the Governor of Northern Ireland was flown at sea for the first time on the Reina del Pacifico.

Launched on September 23, 1930, the Reina made a special guest cruise in the Irish Sea in March, the following year, and then sailed on her maiden voyage from Liverpool to Valparaiso on April 9, 1931. She returned on June 8, having called at 18 ports when outward-bound and at 23 ports on her homeward leg. In spite of the gales encountered, not one case of sea-sickness was reported.

In January, 1932, she arrived at Liverpool having set up a new record by completing her homeward voyage from Valparaiso, via the Panama Canal — a distance of 9,000 miles — in 25 days. And oil was not the only fuel burnt on that exciting round trip — a quarter of a million cigarettes were sold on board!

Of all the famous passengers she carried during her lifetime, one historical name will always be linked with her — that of Mr. Ramsay MacDonald, the former British Prime Minister, who died on board in November, 1937.

Requisitioned as a troopship in 1939, a few days before the war, she found herself in convoy bound for the Far East on September 5. This was the first convoy of the war to steam out from the Clyde into the treacherous Atlantic, and with the Reina were the Duchess of Bedford, Britannic, Montcalm, Scythia, Orion, Orford, Orcades, Strathaird and Clan Ferguson.

Above:
Reina del Pacifico on her first visit to Liverpool in March, 1931.(D.P. & E.)

Below:
The Duke and Duchess of Abercorn went for a six-hour trip in the new Reina del Pacifico, seen here leaving Belfast in March, 1931, on a special-guest cruise in the Irish Sea. (London News Agency)

Reina del Pacifico about to dock at Liverpool in July, 1933, with a fresh breeze on her port beam. (L.N. Winder)

She carried some 150,000 service personnel and sailed 350,000 miles during her wartime career, which included transporting the first Canadian troops to Britain, troops to and from Norway, and acting as an assault ship and commodore ship during the invasions of North Africa, Sicily and Italy. After the Sicily landings, she returned to Liverpool to embark King Peter of Jugoslavia and his staff for Port Said. The King was en route home. Then the Reina went on to Taranto with troops. This voyage was the only one in the four years that Captain C. Stowe had commanded the Reina del Pacifico that the convoy she was in was not attacked.

She had several narrow escapes from being sunk. When successfully landing American troops on "Zebra" Beaches, near Oran, as an assault ship, she was shelled by Axis shore batteries and was hit below the bridge and on the promenade deck. But the most amazing story of this action was that a live shell was shot right through a porthole of her dining-room and out of another on the other side, without exploding!

For their good work at Oran, Captain Stowe received the D.S.C., and Staff Captain R. Bridson and four cadets were all mentioned in dispatches.

While in North Africa, because she was the only vessel left with feeding facilities, the Reina had to supply meals for the crews and troops of 28 other ships. Meals passed through her kitchens for some 1,500 persons in 12 minutes.

During a Merseyside air-raid on April 15/16, 1941, Reina del Pacifico survived "near misses" from many bombs which fell around her — even a large delayed-action bomb, which exploded alongside her, damaging only some crockery! She was also lucky during three nights of bombing at Avonmouth, but when a 1,000 lb. bomb exploded within 20 feet of her when landing troops at Narvik, her bridge and engine-room communications were dislocated. In spite of the damage, she still managed to sail back to the Clyde and then return again to Narvik — this time to help evacuate troops.

German propaganda claimed her sunk in 1942, but the Germans never explained how later she managed to carry hundreds of their compatriots as prisoners of war from North Africa to Britain!

November, 1943, saw the Reina leaving Liverpool for Bombay to take part in the war against the Japanese. Once more, she survived two air attacks on her convoy.

Perhaps the most harrowing operation the Reina del Pacifico carried out in her career was in October, 1944, when she transported some 3,000 Russian prisoners from Italy to Egypt on their way back to Russia. This was no joyful homegoing, with anticipation of a welcome reunion with compatriots and loved ones of the end of the voyage. . . .

Chiefly from Soviet Central Asia, they were probably going to be shot as Red Army deserters. Having been captured by the Germans, they had willingly or, as they all declared, been compelled, to join them in fighting the Allies.

The full story of this otherwise little-known chapter of the last war is told in the book "Naples '44," by Norman Lewis, who accompanied them as a sergeant in British Field Security. Reina del Pacifico carried the prisoners on the first leg of the voyage from Taranto to Port Said, where the prisoners were transhipped to the

Derricks, ropes and shadows weave a spidery sunset pattern about the Reina del Pacifico, loading at North Canada Dock, Liverpool, on January 16, 1934.
(T.W. Hatton)

trooper Devonshire. The Devonshire took them to Khorramshahr, in Iran, where they entrained for Russia. . . in pig-trucks.

At last, in 1946, having well earned her "ticket to Civvy Street", Reina del Pacifico sailed to Belfast for a complete conversion. Although her splendid pre-war furniture (which had been stored in Bootle) was destroyed during the air raids on Merseyside, she was soon her old regal self again. Merseyside applauded her homecoming, dressed in all her queenly regalia. But gladness was also tinged with sorrow following the disastrous explosion which had occurred on board while she was on her refit trials.

Steaming off the Copeland Isles, near Belfast Lough, on September 11, 1947, she suffered a big explosion in her engine-room, which caused the deaths of 28 and injured 23. Many Merseysiders were among the crew, Harland and Wolff and P.S.N.C's technical staff being involved. Four tugs towed the liner back to Belfast, where her exterior, except for a blackened aft funnel, gave little idea of the severe damage below. Captain John Whitehouse, who became Commodore of the P.S.N.C. fleet, said at the time that he thought the ship had struck a mine.

Assisted by the tug, Alfred, the Reina del Pacifico, in July, 1953, prepares to leave the Mersey for yet another voyage to South America. (E. Huxley)

A young Ulsterman, Dr. Edward Hamilton, of Bangor, making his first trip in the Reina del Pacifico as surgeon, was the hero of this tragedy. The only doctor on board, he insisted, in spite of further fire risks, on being lowered into the darkened engine-room, where ladders had been blown to fragments, and waded knee-deep in oil and debris to free seriously-wounded men trapped by twisted and broken metal. With the second-class lounge converted into a sick-bay, and a squad of stewards tearing sheets and tablecloths for bandages, Dr. Hamilton personally dressed the wounds of all the casualties. Later, while serving in the P.S.N.C. liner Orduna, Dr. Hamilton was awarded the M.B.E. for his courageous work in the Pacifico.

A court of inquiry found that the primary explosion was caused by a piston overheating and the inflammable contents of the engine crank cases being ignited.

Reina del Pacifico finally resumed her South American service on October 21, 1948 — more than two years after being released from transport duties. Her second post-war commercial voyage opened up the first British-operated express liner service between the U.K. and Colombia.

Some strange little incidents can creep into a liner's career and, in December, the next year, Reina del Pacifico achieved the somewhat dubious distinction of having carried the first Cuban stowaway to land in Liverpool since the outbreak of the war in 1939. This "honour" was certainly not appreciated by the 19-years-old stowaway who, shivering in the wintry English air, declared that he had wanted to go to Spain and look for work!

Seven mysterious small fires occurred on the liner between January 10 and March 20, 1956, when she was making her round trip with peers, baronets and Merseyside business people among her passengers, most of whom were unaware of the danger. A seaman was later charged and imprisoned.

On July 8, the following year, she hit the world headlines when she ran aground — the full length of her keel — in the notoriously rugged coral-reef area of Devil's Flat, in Bell Channel, off Bermuda. She was stranded for 84 hours. Among her complement of 400 passengers (and 300 crew) were 62 Boy Scouts and Girl Guides, coming to Britain for the World Jamboree at Sutton Coldfield. She was under the command of relief master, Captain Edward C. Hicks, of Exeter, and a Bermudan pilot was also on the bridge.

Fortunately, the liner was not holed, and some 700 tons of cargo, including copper, tin, cotton and motor vehicles were unloaded. A U.S. Coastguard cutter and two local tugs failed to pull her off the bank, so a Constellation aircraft was flown out to Bermuda with 14 tons of salvage equipment.

The "Queen" and her passengers were unruffled and quite secure during the stranding. But to cheer all on board, a Jamaican calypso band sailed out and entertained with the likes of this:

"We all embarked on the Reina
From the beautiful shores of sweet Jamaica
And to our great surprise after a pleasant voyage
Here we are now aground six miles out of Bermuda."

Reina del Pacifico entering Gladstone Dock on July 24, 1957, six days late after becoming stranded on Devil's Flat reef, off Bermuda. (D.P. & E.)

I cannot think what sort of tune fitted such irregular lines, but there it is for the record!

Not to be outdone by the calypsoites, a passenger wrote a poem about the liner's plight. This was so popular that it was circularised within the ship. Two of the verses ran:

> "There she lay by night and by day
> For six and eighty hours;
> A stricken Queen with a starboard lean,
> Bereft of all her powers.

> But we mustn't scoff, for they pulled her off
> With some special salvage gear
> Flown o'er the sea by B.O.A.C.
> And up went a rousing cheer."

Some of the passengers spent the daytime in Bermuda and slept on board. And some of the crew whiled away their leisure hours fishing for sharks. But when ships are delayed, their crews can have problems, too. Assistant chief steward Mr. Reginald Brooks certainly had his. He found himself in a dilemma because he was to

7 a.m. on July 4, 1957, and Captain Edward C. Hicks recounts his story of the Reina's grounding to the author, on the liner's return to Liverpool. His comment: "Heads will roll after this!"

have given away his daughter, Doreen, at her wedding in Liverpool. Reg had to cable the family to go ahead without him. A local councillor stood in for him!

With the help of a high tide and the flown-out tackle, the liner was refloated. Because she had run on to spongy coral, which had moulded itself around her hull, she fortunately was undamaged. Passengers were given the option of flying home, but only 26 Americans on a luxury tour, and 15 others, took advantage of this offer.

Because of the ship's list when stranded, one of the passengers said on return to Liverpool: "We had to learn to live at an angle." The British Ambassador at Bogota, then Mr.James E. Joint, declared: "It was a most pleasant shipwreck! What surprised us most of all was the marvellous service. Within 20 minutes of going on the reef, the stewards were serving morning coffee as usual!"

But the Reina del Pacifico had not completely divorced herself from trouble, and on her next voyage, some hours after leaving Liverpool for the West Indies and South America under her regular master, Captain David Hutchison, she had to put into Milford Haven and then return to her home port with generator trouble. The voyage was cancelled. The liner resumed her sailing schedule again on October 24, but even more bad luck lay in wait . . . . She lost one of her propellers while manoeuvering off Havana on November 10 and this had to be replaced at Balboa, Panama.

In March, 1958. P.S.N.C. announced the Reina del Pacifico's last round trip — from Liverpool to South America and return. When her last passengers disembarked at Liverpool on April 27, they joined hands and sang "Auld Lang Syne". The 27-years-old Reina del Pacifico then remained in the port awaiting her fate.

There was talk of her being offered for sale to Japanese shipbreakers. But she was sold to the British Iron and Steel Corporation and, in May, sailed to the breaker's yard of John Cashmore, Ltd., Newport, Monmouthshire, where her old consort, Orbita, had also ended her days, in 1950.

Reina del Mar

In the story of this ship we see the dying struggles and the frustrations of trying to maintain a passenger-liner service in the face of ever-increasing revenue losses and air-travel supremacy.

Like her elder sister, the Reina del Pacifico, Pacific Steam Navigation's twin-screw, 20,000-ton Reina del Mar was a cosmopolitan vessel, whose launch at Harland and Wolff's Belfast yard on June 7, 1955, was watched by the ambassadors of Colombia, Peru and Ecuador, and the Minister of State for Chile.

And the design of this new queen, able to accommodate 780 passengers in three classes, was very modern compared with her sister. She had a well-raked (and slightly curved), stem and a cruiser stern, and her foremast and single funnel were also distinctive. Eight de-luxe cabins in her first-class accommodation, each named after a particular country served by the liner, were decorated in a manner to depict the characteristics of those countries. Other facilities included excellent restaurants, attractively decorated and comfortable public rooms, open-air swimming pools, children's playrooms and dining-room and a shopping arcade.

Captain George H. Rice, a native of Castletownsend, County Cork, appointed Chief Officer of the Reina del Pacifico in 1940, who commanded many of the company's vessels, and who was appointed Commodore of the fleet in October, 1956, took the new liner on her maiden voyage. This was to Bermuda, Nassau, Havana, Jamaica, Panama, Ecuador, Peru and Chile, on May 3, 1956. He was Chief Officer of the Laguna when she was torpedoed in 1943, and was commended for his services in salvaging her. And, because the Reina's Chief Engineer then was Mr. A. Currie, she was quickly dubbed the "Curry and Rice" liner!

The Chilean press, in February, 1954, had hailed Captain Rice as the "miracle master". For, after 263 train passengers were stranded when heavy rain washed away the railway track between Santiago and Antofagasta, he packed them all into his ship, the Santander — which had accommodation for only a dozen passengers — and carried them to safety.

Reina del Mar was P.S.N.C.'s 13th post-war vessel, but she was certainly not unlucky. This fine ship cost some £5 million and, perhaps, it was in the sad knowledge that the days of the great passenger liners were numbered which prompted the company's managing director, Mr. Leslie Bowes, to say when on the shakedown cruise: "She will make an operational profit, but it is doubtful whether that will cover depreciation."

Reina del Mar entering Sandon Basin, Liverpool in April, 1956, to prepare for her maiden voyage.

Reina del Mar, resplendent with white hull and buff funnel, and the largest ship P.S.N.C. had owned, arrived at Liverpool for the first time on April 9, 1956. Her pre-maiden voyage trip to Scotland's Western Isles on April 20 was a three-day champagne-and-caviare cruise for special guests. These included General Sir Brian Robertson, chairman of the British Transport Commission, Dr. Pedro Pereira, the Portuguese Ambassador, and the Lord Mayor of Liverpool (Ald. Reginald Bailey). This was also the occasion when one of the welcome, but uninvited, passengers found that, like time and tide, liners are demons for punctuality, too.

. . . . As Mr. Bill Urmston learned when the Reina del Mar carried him with her from Liverpool on that Scottish cruise. Bill was certainly not "here for the beer". He merely had to arrange a window display in the liner's shopping arcade. And, that night, he should have been at his Little Sutton, Wirral, home, celebrating his wife's 29th birthday! (Something similar to this shanghaing-with-a-difference was related in the Empress of Britain III story).

Ships, as sailors will tell you, are "living" things, sometimes with other than sea duties to perform. And so, Reina del Mar, freshly returned from the Western Isles, had yet another bow to take before her Merseyside public in advance of her maiden voyage. Like other

139

The Reina del Mar making her first passenger voyage from Liverpool on Friday, April 20, 1956. This was a special-guest cruise to Scotland's Western Isles, under the command of Captain G.H. Rice. It was also the same day that the new Empress of Britain (III) made her maiden voyage from Liverpool to Canada. Reina del Mar made her maiden voyage from Liverpool to the West Indies and South America a few days later, on May 3. (D.P. & E.)

Liverpool-based liners often were, she became the venue of a big social function. This was a charity ball in aid of the Child Welfare Association. Numbers were restricted to 300, and they will remember this virgin sea queen with great affection for they were honoured and privileged guests to have been given the use of a brand-new liner for this good cause.

On Thursday, May 3, Reina del Mar's great day arrived. Dressed overall, gleaming white in the early summer sunshine, she moved out, stern first, from Liverpool's Prince's Stage to start her maiden voyage. Salutes of sirens and shrill whistles bade her bon voyage as she headed for the Bar, the Irish Sea and the North Atlantic Ocean.

Although then a dying breed, the liners of Liverpool still merited absolute respect and V.I.P. treatment. So, it was only to be expected that the Post Office sanctioned the use of a commemorative date-stamp to cancel mail posted on board the Reina del Mar that voyage. She called at some 38 ports during her 65-day round trip from Liverpool to the West Coast of South America, and no one was more pleased with the "Queen's" performance than Captain Rice. "She handles beautifully and steers like a yacht, even with her engines stopped," he said, on her return to Liverpool on July 7.

Reina del Mar continued to operate with the Reina del Pacifico as her consort until the latter was sold for scrap in 1958. The del Mar then was the only big passenger liner on the U.K./West Coast of South America service.

Shortly before Christmas, 1956, the Reina del Mar answered an urgent radio message to help an injured Greek seaman on board the freighter, Ocean Wave, west of the Azores. The sea was so rough that some of the Reina's crew physically had to snatch the stretchered man from a long boat as it rose on the crest of a wave! He was brought to Liverpool where he recovered from a suspected fractured skull.

Fidel Castro's take-over of Cuba severely hit the Reina del Mar in 1960, when she could no longer make her usual calls at the ports there. About a third of the ship's revenue was thus lost.

Early 1962 saw her introducing the first fast regular passenger service between Liverpool and Trinidad, but still continuing to call at Chile and Peru. She also cruised that year to the Mediterranean on charter to the newly-formed Travel Savings Limited, the cut-price cruise organisation, founded by millionaire Mr. Max Wilson. In October, 1962, P.S.N.C. announced cruising plans for the following year, with fares as low as $2\frac{1}{2}$d a sea mile. The 215 economy-class passengers would enjoy all the usual amenities of the ship, including shore excursions.

Reina del Mar seemed to have had quite a friendly relationship with railway people and, on March 9, 1963, P.S.N.C. welcomed on board the liner two Liverpool railmen for some first-class treatment. On January 3, diesel-electric locomotive driver Mr. Fred Hitchmough and his second man, Mr. Ted Moore, had brought their train, full of anxious potential passengers, ready to embark on the Reina del Mar, from London to Liverpool through fog, snow and ice. No one thought that they could do it. It was a vicious winter day and there were bad traffic hold-ups all over the country. But Fred and Ted battled on. They were 81 minutes late as they pulled into Riverside Station, but their passengers caught their ship. Deservedly, the men and their families were feted on board the Reina del Mar when she returned to Liverpool.

The Reina made her first cruise to pioneer cheap holiday travel when she left the Mersey on the overcast Bank Holiday week-end of August, 1963, bound for the Mediterranean with 570 passengers, half of whom had paid between £50 and £60 for the fortnight's voyage in the sun. But plans were in hand to transfer the liner to the Travel Savings Association (T.S.A.).

The next month, September, it was announced that Mr. Wilson's T.S.A. was to buy its first ship — the Reina del Mar — from P.S.N.C., now a subsidiary of Royal Mail Lines. The deal would be made through a yet-to-be formed company, a subsidiary of T.S.A., and Royal Mail would retain an interest in the liner. Purchase price and the cost of the liner's anticipated renovation would be more than £3 million.

T.S.A. had earlier chartered not only the Reina, but the Empress of Britain and the Empress of England.

Reina del Mar being towed stern first from Prince's Landing Stage, Liverpool, at the start of her maiden voyage to South America on Thursday, May 3, 1956. (D.P. & E.)

Reina del Mar would not be taken over by T.S.A. until her 1963 schedule was completed, plus her special 64-day winter cruise to Florida the next January. Merseyside was about to suffer the loss of yet another of her liners. Although pride in the Reina ran high locally, the real concern was for the diminishing sea-faring jobs. Of the Reina's 350 crew, 280 were British, many of them Merseysiders, and the remainder, Spanish.

P.S.N.C. said in September, 1963, that they saw no difficulty in absorbing those not required by T.S.A., and Mr. J.J. Gawne, the company's managing director, who later became chairman, declared the company's intention of modifying at least nine of their current cargo-passenger ships to make up for the reduced passenger accommodation previously afforded by the Reina del Mar. The company fought hard to hold the still-young vessel and appealed to the Government for a grant to help keep this, their last passenger liner, operational. Mr. Gawne then explained: "Both the Foreign Secretary and the Minister of Transport have studied the matter and agree that the Reina del Mar is a symbol of British craftsmanship, but they cannot make any exceptions for one unit . . . ." T.S.A. took over the Reina del Mar in October, that year, as their first ship, although P.S.N.C. still had an interest in her, and she was managed by Union Castle.

A surprise announcement from Sir Nicholas Cayzer, then chairman of Travel Savings Limited, on November 3, 1963, declared that Reina del Mar was to be sold to a Greek shipping company. She would continue to sail as a cruise liner but on charter to Travel Savings under the Greek flag and with a Greek crew. Sir Nicholas explained that Travel Savings Limited, primarily a sales organisation and not a shipping company, was not geared to operating a cruise ship on a complicated itinerary. The organisation, therefore, had decided to sell the vessel to the Greek company associated with the Chandris Group, but the ship would be chartered for her lifetime to T.S.L.

This disclosure brought cries of protest from the Seamen's Union and the Merchant Navy and Airline Officers' Association. The general secretary of the N.U.S., then Mr. William Hogarth, said: "Here is a clear case for Government action to halt such sales of British ships abroad for use in competition with our own ships. At first glance, this is tantamount to condoning flags of convenience."

The MN and ACA were bitter, too. Said their spokesman: ". . . a statement of this kind, put out by a British organisation, which has three leading British shipowners as its backers, will suggest to British 'seagoers and the public generally that British shipowners are lacking in abilities and are slipping from their leading positions in the world . . . ."

Whether this outburst had any effect is not recorded but at the start of the New Year, 1964, P.S.N.C. announced that the Reina del Mar would not be sold to the Greeks. Instead, she would be sold to a new consortium, comprised of P.S.N.C. (with a holding of 25 per cent), Canadian Pacific, British and Commonwealth Shipping (Clan Line and the Union Castle Group) and Max Wilson's Travel Savings Association. The liner had been incurring losses on the West Coast of South America passenger service, running between £200,000 and £300,000 a year, and in her eight years at sea, she had never made a profit.

With Captain D. Idris Jones (who had been commanding her for nearly two years), she made her last scheduled voyage — a winter cruise — in this service from Liverpool on January 2, 1964. This was

A striking picture of the Reina del Mar in more than one sense. She is tied up at Prince's Landing Stage in June, 1960 – during a shipping strike!

historic in that, although P.S.N.C. would continue to operate a passenger service to Spain, Portugal, the West Indies, Panama and the Pacific Coast of South America, in small numbers in their cargo vessels, Reina del Mar would be their last luxury liner on a service which had linked Liverpool with South America for nearly a century.

It is quite astounding how a ship can win so many admirers, and this queen of the sea had thousands of devoted subjects in all her many ports of call. Homeward-bound on her previous voyage, South Americans and Spaniards had virtually queued for hours to wave and to shout their farewells to this liner — "Pacifico's sister" — which they had come to love in such a relatively short time. The Mayor of Cartegena, Chile, and his civic entourage, turned out at 7.30 a.m. to present Reina del Mar's Commodore-Captain with the freedom of the city. Deputations and farewell presentations greeted her at all the ports.

Reina del Mar had been born into an age when air travel was rapidly becoming favoured and the era of the big liners was passing. A new age was developing when it was "quick transit gloriously" — on "Mondays" or any other day! As P.S.N.C. archivist, John

Destined to become a full-time cruise liner, Reina del Mar displays her changed profile. (Travel Savings Limited)

Lingwood, aptly put it: "The sonic boom of jet travel sounded the death-knell of passage by sea."

Reina del Mar was one of the last of the Liverpool liners and, like the Reina del Pacifico, she was also built as "an act of faith" which, sadly, was not to be realised. Destined to become a full-time cruise liner, the Reina was returned to her builders, Harland and Wolff, for a 13-week refit in March, 1964. She had such a face-lift that her profile was changed, and the forward lounge on the promenade deck was extended forward and to the ship's sides, making it one of the biggest lounges in any liner. The forward restaurant, once seating 200, now seated 412, and an entirely new cinema and sun-deck were constructed. Her houseflag was that of "TSL" in gold on a background of royal blue, and she returned to Liverpool to prepare for the first of three cruises to America under that flag that summer.

Although her links with South America were broken, Reina del Mar continued to keep her passengers in the lap of luxury and her name rang as regally as ever as she carried on cruising for the Travel Savings Association. But even the liner's new owners could not change her fortune overnight. As early as October, 1963, T.S.A. had had to call off what had promised to be a popular transatlantic parade-of-the-pops cruise from Liverpool to New York, scheduled for the following July.

The liner was to have sailed with 800 jazz fans on a £56 minimum, 19-day trip to New York. But the company was stuck with bookings for only 100 on the 800-berth ship. Top British bands and artistes were to have appeared in cabaret in America, and the passengers, drawn from British jazz clubs, were to have seen and heard the great bands of America at the New York World Fair.

A "one-night stand" in the shape of another charity ball, attended by over 400 on board the liner that October was a resounding success. Organised by the Liverpool regional committee of the Variety Club of Great Britain, the facilities afforded by the "sea queen" were ideal for the Latin-American ball, held while the liner was in Canada Dock, in aid of under-privileged children and young people. Several of the city's South American consuls and their wives attended to dance to Edmundo Ros and his Band.

Some 700 passengers booked for her first T.S.A. cruise from Liverpool on June 10, 1964, under the command of Captain John James. On an 18-day cruise, the tourist fares were between £45 and £75, and passengers had the opportunity of visiting the New York World Fair in the four days that the liner served as their floating hotel in the port.

She made her fastest turn-round when she departed for New York on her second cruise on June 28, 1964, in $13\frac{1}{2}$ hours after her return to Liverpool. A small army of cleaners and stewards worked like beavers through the ship, preparing the cabins and the public rooms for some 900 passengers, including holiday parties from Scandinavia. A spokesman for the Mersey Docks and Harbour Board commented: "As far as the Prince's Landing Stage is concerned, that is the fastest turn-round ever done, remembering that no cargo was taken on board, only passengers' baggage and supplies."

August 27 that year saw her sailing from Liverpool to Japan, via South Africa and Singapore. At Yokohama she was used again as a floating hotel for T.S.A. members for the whole period of the Olympic Games. Homeward-bound, she called at Hong Kong, with two days ashore for passengers, and at Penang and Mauritius. Using Capetown as a base, she then made a series of cruises from South Africa and — a sign of the times and an indication of future cruise-liner policy — arrangements were made for passengers to join or leave the ship by air during her itinerary.

Reina del Mar continued to operate as a cruise liner but in September, 1973, she was bought outright by the Union Castle Line. She took that line's colours and was based at Southampton as a permanent cruise ship. She made her first cruise to the Caribbean under her new owners, and same name, that autumn. This proved so successful that a further 29-day cruise was planned for 1974, plus another dozen cruises out of Southampton.

But, halfway through 1974, the world was informed that Reina del Mar was to be withdrawn from service the following April, after

Reina del Mar, pictured in Union Castle Line livery, always received a great welcome at her many ports of call.
(British and Commonwealth Shipping Co. Ltd.)

completing her cruising programme. She was, once again, the victim of "increased operational costs", particularly in fuel oil and in crew.

With talk of demolition in the wind, it was hard to realise that this ship, which had cost £5 million to build and £3 million to refit, even after 18 years, was then worth less than £1 million as scrap. Someone suggested that she should become a floating hostel for London students, but this idea fell through and, in May, 1975, she was broken up.

Some Famous "Shire" Ships

"Every Sunday evening we still sing 'Eternal Father strong to save,' and pray for those in peril on the sea. Some might dismiss this as an old-fashioned, outworn custom. But today we are faced with the fact that there are still those in peril on the sea . . . ."

These poignant words were spoken by the Rector of Liverpool, the Rev. Donald Gray, of the "Sailors' Church" of Our Lady and St. Nicholas, at Liverpool's Pier Head, on October 16, 1980. He was addressing some 2,000 mourners gathered at the city's Anglican Cathedral for a special service to the memory of the crew of 42, who all perished when the giant iron-ore carrier, Derbyshire, sank without trace in the Pacific the previous month. Among the crew of the Derbyshire (ex-Liverpool Bridge), a victim of Typhoon Orchid when on passage to Japan, were 17 Merseysiders.

The disaster served to remind us that even in this modern age of technical wonders, and in peacetime, too, the sea can be the eternal enemy against which there can never be any relaxing of vigilance. Although this massive 169,080 ton deadweight Bibby Line oil-bulk-ore carrier was not a passenger liner, she hailed from Liverpool's oldest independent shipping company (1805), which has produced numerous liners and troopships during its long existence.

Famous for its service to the Mediterranean and the East Indies, Bibby's accrued a wealth of trooping experience from its participation in the Crimean War, the South African War and the two World Wars. (The peacetime livery of all chartered British troopships was white, with a broad blue band around the hull and a yellow funnel).

One of the company's best-known ships was the first Oxfordshire, a hospital ship in both world wars.

Built as an 8,648-ton passenger liner by Harland and Wolff, Belfast, in 1912 (about the same time as the Titanic), she operated between London, Liverpool and Rangoon. At the outbreak of the Great War, she was the first British merchant ship to be requisitioned and, fitted out as a hospital, the first to serve with the Grand Fleet. But after a very short time she returned to act as a hospital ship for the armies in France and Belgium, ferrying wounded across the Channel. Later, she took part in the Dardenelles campaign and played an active role in the evacuation of the wounded in 1915.

In 1916, she returned to the English Channel and later sailed to the Aegean Sea and the Persian Gulf to help the wounded in the Salonika and Mesopotamia campaigns. From the end of 1916 to 1918, she served with the East African Expedition. Converted to oil-burning after the war and refurbished for passenger and cargo-carrying, she

Oxfordshire (I) served as a hospital ship in both world wars.   (Bibby Line)

returned to the Rangoon service and continued this operation until 1939.

During the inter-wars period, when many shipping ventures failed, in addition to trading, Bibby's also had the benefit of trooping contracts which ran continously from 1921 to 1939. Then, of course, their ships were virtually swallowed up by trooping demands.

At the outbreak of the last war, when she was the oldest vessel in the Bibby Line fleet, Oxfordshire was called on once more to fulfil duties as a hospital ship. She served as a base hospital at Freetown, in the Mediterranean and in the Far East. Oxfordshire also saw service at the North Africa landings and later evacuated 700 wounded Americans from the Anzio beach-head. She also served for two months in the Adriatic. The first British hospital ship to visit Australia, she was also the first to serve with the British Pacific Fleet, arriving at Leyte weeks before the other British floating hospitals.

Arriving at Liverpool on December 5, 1945, she brought 386 passengers from the Far East. Among them were 40 missionaries released from Japanese camps in China. Some of these had spent up to nine years in captivitiy, having been incarcerated in the early days of the Japanese occupation of China.

She continued to serve as a hospital ship until July, 1948, when her fitments were stripped, cabins and public rooms renovated and rearranged, and her engines overhauled. She emerged, ready to

Last of Bibby Line's traditional old-time liners, the once four-masted, 11,600-ton Derbyshire is pictured in 1948, reconditioned, with two masts and a squat funnel. She helped to re-establish the company's pre-war service between Britain and Burma. During the war, Derbyshire was an armed merchant cruiser and a troop transport, carrying landing craft. She steamed 330,000 miles and carried 136,000 troops during her wartime service. (Bibby Line)

accommodate 668 passengers. For many months she carried emigrants and displaced persons to Australia and then, in 1951, aged 39, she was sold to the Pan-Islamic Steamship Company, of Karachi, for service as the pilgrim ship, Safina El Arab. She was finally broken up in 1958 at the ripe old age of 46.

Last of Bibby's traditional old-time liners was the graceful 11,600-ton, single-funnelled, four-masted motorship, Derbyshire II. Built by Fairfield's, of Govan, and launched on June 10, 1935, she made her maiden voyage from Liverpool to Rangoon on November 8. A one-class ship, she originally carried 291 passengers and a crew of 224.

Among her excellent facilities — particularly suited for Indian Ocean service — was an outdoor swimming pool, surrounded by cubicles with fresh-water showers. During the ensuing war she became, in turn, an armed merchant cruiser, troopship, headquarters ship and assault ship, serving in the North African, Italian, Southern France and Far East invasions. She steamed 330,000 miles on war service and carried more that 136,000 troops.

In January, 1945, she arrived at Rangoon, the first allied ship to reach Burma after the Japanese occupation. At the liberation of Singapore, as a headquarters ship to which the captured Japanese commander had to report daily, she also provided hundreds of ex-prisoners of war with their first "homelike" meals for several years!

Returned to the Bibby line in November, 1946, she was the first of the fleet to be reconverted for peacetime duties. The Worcestershire and the Staffordshire followed. She underwent an extensive refit at Govan and emerged a much-changed shape. Three of her masts were removed, the foremast remaining, and she was given a new stepped mizzen mast and a shorter, wider funnel. Her superstructure was also shortened, which made her appear more squat.

Six other "shire" liners were operating for the company at this time and although business was brisk for a period, increasing air-travel and the independence of Burma in 1948, saw a gradual waning of passenger traffic. A service continued to be maintained for several more years but the passenger traffic finally ceased in 1965. Staffordshire was sold for scrap in 1959. Worcestershire in 1961, and the Derbyshire, aged 29, was also sold in 1964 for breaking up in the Far East.

In 1966, another Derbyshire was built — a 14,000-ton deadweight general cargo ship, which was sold in 1974. Her name was taken by the Liverpool Bridge in 1977, when the latter left the Seabridge consortium and returned to the Bibby service. She was the ship lost in the 1980 typhoon tragedy.

Bibby's last troop transport, Oxfordshire the second, was launched at Govan on December 15, 1955. The Government had asked for a long-term contract for Oxfordshire to operate alongside the Devonshire, built in 1939. But, because of work pressure, she

Oxfordshire (II), Bibby's largest and last troop transport, later became the Fairstar and carried emigrants to Australia. (Bibby Line)

151

The Devonshire, built in 1939 as a troopship, saw service in every theatre of the last world war. (Bibby Line)

could not be delivered until 1957, and she made her maiden voyage on February 28 that year, from Liverpool to Hong Kong.

At 20,568 tons, she was almost twice the size of any ship ever built for Bibby's up to that time. She managed 17 knots, carried 220 first-class passengers, 100 second-class and 180 third-class, plus 1,000 on the troopdecks, and a crew of 368. Because she had messes, armouries, a quartermaster's store, ammunition rooms and canteen, she was described as a "floating Aldershot".

Oxfordshire and British India Company's new troopship, the Nevassa (20,527), were the largest vessels ever built solely for trooping purposes.

But the Oxfordshire was never fully utilised and, in 1958, trooping was discontinued from Liverpool, where troops had embarked since the war. Both she and the Devonshire were transferred to Southampton. At the end of 1962, Oxfordshire's and Devonshire's trooping days were over. The Government had decided to give up sea-trooping with the end of National Service and to economise generally on this front. The Devonshire was sold in 1962 to British India Steam Navigation Company. Renamed the Devonia, she served as an educational ship and was broken up in 1968. In 1964, the Oxfordshire was sold to Sitmar as the Fairstar and carried emigrants on assisted passages from Southampton to Australia.

When the last Oxfordshire (the third), another giant of 19,000 tons, was built in 1971 at Sunderland, Bibby Line had been out of the passenger market for some ten years and was concentrating on the charter markets. Oxfordshire, able to accommodate 1,800 saloon cars, was sold to Marsenorio Armadara and renamed Georgios Tzakiroglou. She carried cars from Japan to the U.S.A. and returned with bulk cargoes.

Vandyck, Vasari, Vestris and Voltaire

Lamport and Holt's V-class ships were popular passenger-cargo liners which were part of the Merseyside scene before the Great War and up to the early part of the last war. Names like Vandyck, Voltaire, Vauban and Vestris were particularly well known.

The fleet of Lamport and Holt (now part of the Vestey Group), dates from the middle of the last century, when the company established trade between Britain and the east coast of South America. Its V-liners were first introduced with the 7,542-ton Velasquez and the 7,877-ton Veronese, both built in 1906, the former at Middlesborough and the latter at Belfast. They were wrecked early in their careers. Two popular liners in this class were the Vandyck (the third) and the second Voltaire, launched at Belfast, respectively, on February 24, 1921, and August 14, 1923. At 13,233 tons, Vandyck accommodated 680 passengers — 300 first-class, 150 second-class and 230 third-class. Her sister, with the same displacement, also carried this number of passengers.

Many famous people travelled in these ships, among whom were Sir Ernest Shackleton, the polar explorer, and Anna Pavlova, the ballerina. Theodore (Teddy) Roosevelt, the President of the U.S.A. and also a keen explorer, always sailed in one of the V-liners from New York, when travelling south on some of his hunting trips.

The Vandyck, dressed overall in her "glory" days.   (J.S. Clarkson)

153

Delius, in the Mersey off New Brighton. She was the first vessel to be destroyed by a glider-bomb. (J.S. Clarkson)

Mr. Frederick Page, of Wallasey, Merseyside, who served with Lamport and Holt for 52 years — mostly at sea — worked on the ships which operated a passenger-cargo service between North and South America. He recalls how the berth the liners used in New York was dubbed 'Millionaires' Pier'. "We carried the cream of America's wealthy society, and many V.I.P.s, who were going south in those days," he said. "The pier from which they embarked had accommodation and facilities which were the last word in luxury."

But there were no millionaires with Fred and his colleagues on Lamport and Holt's 6,000-ton cargo ship, Delius, when she was bombed at sea in November, 1943. Delius was the first vessel to be attacked by a "glider-bomb," which killed her master, Captain J.H. George, of Childwall, Liverpool, and three of the crew.

Delius' steering gear was smashed and a fire started in one of her holds as she sailed in convoy near Gibraltar, returning from India. Listing badly from the weight of water pumped into the hold to barely keep the fire in check, the survivors, "steering by the stars," for ten days, finally made Glasgow. Five Merseyside members of her crew, including Mr. Page (the boatswain, who was awarded the B.E.M.), received decorations and commendations for their courageous work in very dangerous circumstances.

Vandyck and Voltaire served for some time between New York and the River Plate, until withdrawn in July, 1930, because of the recession in the passenger trade — and the adverse publicity the company received when another popular V-class liner, the Vestris, sank with great loss of life. Many of the V-fleet suffered various disasters of shipwreck and destruction by enemy action, but the Vestris tragedy — in between the wars — was the worst. The 10,499-

An artist's impression of the ill-fated Vestris. (Craig Carter)

ton sister ship of the Vauban, she sank in a storm off the North American coast on November 12, 1928, with the loss of 112 souls, while sailing between New York, Barbados and Beunos Aires. She carried 129 passengers and 197 crew. Of 37 women on board, only eight were saved. All of the 12 children, also on board, were drowned.

Some of the survivors floated in their life-jackets in warm, shark-infested waters for almost 24 hours before being picked up. Bodies, minus limbs, were seen.

A dramatic incident of the disaster (as reported by the American Press, after the survivors were landed at New York) was given by Captain Frederick Sorenson, sailing as a passenger in the Vestris. He told of "a scene of indescribable horror," when the order was given to abandon ship . . . . "The lifeboats were still about 15 feet above the water when two cracked like eggshells against the ship's side," he said. "The boats broke open and poured their human freight, including many young children, into the sea."

Another witness said that two lifeboats (presumably the same ones) containing women and children, could not be freed. Huge waves smashed them against the ship and they went down with the Vestris.

Second Officer of the Vestris, Mr. Leslie Watson said that when the ship sank, he and the liner's master, Captain William J. Carey, of Waterloo, Liverpool, were holding on to each other. Just before Captain Carey (wearing his heavy overcoat and no life-jacket) drowned, he gasped: "My God, my God, I am not to blame for this!"

There was considerable ill-feeling in America over this tragic affair and some of the newspapers there certainly stirred it up. One carried the headline: "Crew Let Women Die In Boats". Another went so far as to publish a full-page sketch depicting women swimming alongside the wreck among huge, man-eating sharks. One of the latter was shown about to seize a terror-stricken mother with a baby in her arms!

Four black survivors of the Vestris were quickly snapped up by show promoters when they landed in the U.S. — to relate their experiences to theatre audiences. One of them appeared at every performance at four of the big New York theatres. The others, from Barbados, signed a contract to tour the country for 13 guineas each a week.

Two public inquiries into the disaster were held in America, where it was said that the loss was caused by the incompetence of master and crew. The British inquiry, however, which lasted a record 40 days (three days longer than the Titanic inquiry) was more generous to Captain Carey in its findings. Mr. W.K. Raeburn, counsel for the Board of Trade, said that Captain Carey was a man of very great bravery, without whose example the passengers could have panicked.

Some of the contributory causes of the sinking, said the tribunal, were overloading; the tender condition of the ship; insufficient margin of stability and reserve of bouyancy; the half-doors on the upper deck were not weathertight, and the weather-deck hatches were not battened down. And the S.O.S. was sent out six hours too late. In spite of earlier protests from some of the survivors, the lifeboats were found seaworthy. The officers of the Vestris and a company official were blamed for dereliction of duty, but the company was found blameless.

Following this, the New York passenger service was discontinued. Vandyck, Voltaire and Vauban were brought home and laid up. In the spring of 1932, Vandyck and Voltaire were refurbished for cruising. Vauban was broken up.

These cruises, from Liverpool and Southampton, were popular and successful. The now white-painted liners were generally well booked for voyages to a wide variety of ports, including some in North Africa, the Mediterranean, the Atlantic Islands, Portugal, Spain, Norway and the Baltic. Their special features included windows or portholes in every room (the saloon-deck portholes, 20 feet above the waterline, could be opened when at sea); spacious public rooms and verandah cafes; six deck tennis courts; two open-air bathing-pools; a large gymnasium, shops; an orchestra — not to mention "exceptional steadiness at sea"!

Above:
Painters give the Vandyck a change of dress. (Lamport and Holt)

Below:
Tugs assist Vandyck at Prince's Landing Stage, Liverpool.
(Merseyside Maritime Museum)

Company archivist for Lewis's departmental stores, Mr. Mike Benson told me that, so far as he knew, Vandyck was the only ship with a Lewis's shop on board.

"A Miss Gordon used to run this shop right up to the outbreak of the war", he said. "She was not very popular with the Liverpool store's sales managers because she had the authority to go to any department and take away, on transfer, the merchandise she needed for her floating shop.

"Equally, if any of the merchandise remained unsold at the end of a voyage, she could return it to the managers who had to accept it. They did not like this because often, with the movements of the ship, some of the merchandise became 'ship-soiled'!"

Everton F.C. with some of the officers of the liner Vandyck, which they visited at the request of the Staff Captain, a keen Everton supporter, when playing at Tenerife in the summer of 1934.

The late Bill "Dixie" Dean, who led this fabulous team, told me that for the three friendly (but tough) matches they played in the Canary Islands that summer, they had to wear goloshes!

"Perfectly true", said Dixie. "The ground had no grass and was so hard that we couldn't possibly play in studs. So, Mr. Jack Sharp (a club director and founder of the Liverpool sports outfitters more than 80 years ago), had the goloshes prepared for us in advance."

Back row (l to r): Willie Cook, and Officer, Jim Stein, Jack Cunliffe, Cliff Britton, Ben Williams, Charlie Gee, Warney Cresswell. Centre: Albert Geldard, Dixie Dean, Staff Captain H.E. Morrison, Captain Symons, Dr. Cecil Baxter (director of the club), and two officers. Front: an officer, Alec Stevenson, "Miss Lee", Norman Higham and Jack Coulter.

Everton, who went out there in the Dunbar Castle, was the first Football League team to visit the Canary Islands. (D.P. & E.)

A memorable cruise recorded by Voltaire in the 1930's was the Advertising Association's 12th Annual Convention, from July 4 to July 17, to Copenhagen, Stockholm, Helsinki and Oslo, with practically everybody who was anybody in the field of British advertising. Another cruise (in company with the Vandyck), was from Liverpool to Spithead to take part with other Liverpool ships, in the Coronation Royal Naval Review on May 20, 1937.

In 1937, the Vandyck was refitted as a permanent cruise liner. Her hull was painted white, with blue boot topping and a thin black riband at shelter-deck level. She was judged to be a very handsome vessel and the cruises proved to be popular and successful.

Voltaire made some maritime history and achieved a signal honour for Lamport and Holt on July 2, 1932, when she was permitted by Liverpool Corporation to fly as a jack, the city's civic flag — the coat of arms on a plain blue background. This privilege was eventually extended to all the L + H ships, which are still known in eastern South American ports as "The Liverpool Line". It is thought that the Lord Mayor of Liverpool made the local gesture, at a time of world-wide depression, in recognition of the company's part in maintaining trade for the Port of Liverpool. Although this custom was then unique to one shipping line in Britain, a number of German ports also permitted certain German passenger liners to fly their respective ports' civic emblems.

But for being a slower ship, Vandyck might well have become the first British ship to be torpedoed in the last world war. She left Liverpool at 4 p.m. on Saturday, September 2, 1939, bound for New York and carrying Continental refugees. The ill-fated Athenia left Liverpool a little later on the same route, overhauled Vandyck and caught that first torpedo from U.30, fired on the following Sunday evening.

Lamport and Holt's fleet suffered severe losses in the last war, when most of their 21 ships were destroyed. These included the cruising sisters, Vandyck and Voltaire. Vandyck, requisitioned as an armed boarding vessel, was bombed and sunk on June 10, 1940, while on her way to embark Allied troops being evacuated from Norway. Her bell now hangs in the village of Bleik. Seven lost their lives, and her remaining 29 officers and 132 ratings were taken prisoner by the Germans.

Both ships were commandeered by the Admiralty and converted for troop-carrying long before the outbreak of war. On passage from India, returning soldiers and their families to Britain, Voltaire received warning that war was imminent.

She discharged her passengers at Southampton and sailed almost immediately for Scapa Flow, to serve as a hostel ship for the armed services. Fate decreed that she was present there, for when the Royal

Oak was sunk, within a day or two of her arrival, she was able to take the survivors on board.

The following night, in another air-raid, the Iron Duke, anchored almost by her side, was bombed and had to be beached. Voltaire survived some near misses in that raid but sustained only slight damage. The next day, she was renamed Iron Duke (II), to replace the original warship. Later that year she was refitted and converted into an armed merchant cruiser, to become H.M.S. Voltaire. Captain V.E. Gore Hickman, Voltaire's master for most or all of her cruising years, was still with her at Scapa Flow.

Voltaire made patrols in the Mediterranean and acted as an escort to North Atlantic convoys, but her luck ran out on April 9, 1941. She put up a brave fight with the German commerce-raider, Thor, when on route from Trinidad to Freetown for a convoy, but the enemy sank her after a two-hour battle and the 197 survivors were captured as prisoners of war.

The Voltaire at Gladstone Dock in the 1930's.
(Merseyside Maritime Museum)

Although we are primarily talking about the 1930's Voltaire and Vandyck, which were probably the best-known V-liners on Merseyside, I think mention should be made of the 10,000-ton Vasari, which survived to reach the remarkable age of 70. Vasari was built by Sir Raylton Dixon and Company, of Middlesborough, in 1909, for the Liverpool, Brazil and River Plate Steam Navigation

Company, managed by Lamport and Holt, of Liverpool. She served with other V-liners between New York and the River Plate and after the Great War, from 1919 to 1921, with the Vestris and the Vauban, she made about half a dozen voyages from Liverpool to New York for the Cunard Company.

Following the Vestris disaster in 1928, Vasari was sold by Lamport and Holt to a Hull company, converted into a fish-factory ship and renamed Arctic Queen. The Russians then bought her in 1935 and, using her for the same purpose, renamed her Pischevayia Industriya. Thereafter, little or nothing was heard of her and, in about 1960, when it was not certain whether she was still afloat, her name was removed from Lloyd's Register.

She became a "forgotten" ship, until the Iron Curtain suddenly lifted in 1979 and the old Vasari sailed into Hong Kong harbour to anchor and be recognised. But this was her final bow for, a few weeks later, she was towed to Taiwan and broken up.

Vandyck leaving Liverpool for the last summer cruise, in October, 1934. The Canadian Pacific liner, Montclare, can be seen in mid-river, right.(D.P. & E.)

Aba

The story of the Liverpool liners will never be told completely . . . so many ships, so many companies, so many men and so many incidents . . . it is impossible to record them all. But, in conclusion, I must mention some of the famous passenger liners which were part of Elder Dempster's busy fleet, plying between Britain and West Africa.

I have deliberately used this distinguished company to wind up these stories of the Liverpool liners because Elder Dempster's flagship, the Aureol, was the last regular one to operate from the Port of Liverpool. Her story, with brief reference to her sisters, Accra and Apapa, is told in the next and final chapter.

Elder Dempster, which became a subsidiary of Ocean Transport and Trading in 1965, has been an integral part of Merseyside's maritime history from the time that its little paddle steamers butted their way up the malarial Niger two lifetimes ago. Although so many of Elder Dempster's vessels were lost in the two world wars, one of them, the Aba, saw some incredible action in the last war and was the company's only passenger liner to survive it.

As the hospital ship HMHS 34, Aba brought wounded out of Norway, Libya, Greece, Crete and Italy, and was involved in some of the fiercest bombing inflicted by the Axis on our ships in the Mediterranean. Nearly all her crew were Merseyside men. One of them, Mr. Joe Grunnill, of Pensby, Wirral, told me how the liner left Liverpool for Alexandria on what was supposed to be a three-week voyage, and did not get back until three years later!

Originally called Glenapp, the Aba was completed in Glasgow in 1918 for the Glen Line. Elder Dempster bought her a couple of years later and renamed her Aba. She was the first motor passenger liner in the world to be placed in commission, and everything on board "from cleaning knives to scrambling eggs", was performed by electricity. A vessel of 8,000 tons, she carried some 350 passengers on her regular voyages between Liverpool and West Africa in the 1920's and 1930's.

Requisitioned as a hospital ship at the outbreak of the last war, she sailed from Liverpool on September 9, 1939, for Scapa Flow, under Captain W. Dennitts, who remained her master until Spring, 1941. She was put to use at Scapa Flow very quickly, aiding the survivors of the British battleship, Royal Oak, torpedoed by the notorious Captain Gunther Prien in U.47, after he daringly entered this vital naval base on October 14. Twenty-four officers and 809 men of her company perished in this great warship, which turned turtle. Returning to Liverpool, Aba was fitted out in 1940 as a fully-equipped military hospital ship and she sailed to Norway to bring out the sick and wounded.

Aba, the only Elder Dempster passenger liner to survive the last world war. As a hospital ship, she was involved in some of the fiercest bombing on Allied ships in the Mediterranean. Aba is seen here, before the war, tied up at Prince's Landing Stage, Liverpool. (D.P. & E.)

At Piraeus, when Greece was being invaded by the Germans, she took on board 800 wounded and 150 nurses. As the last ship to leave that battered port, she had to run the gauntlet of bombs. While anchored off Canea, Crete, she was raked by aerial machine-guns, and, in May, 1941, an Italian bomber laid a stick of bombs very close to her while she was sailing alone.

Later the same day, sailing in convoy to Alexandria, Aba was bombed by eight Stukas, which came screaming out of the sky. Their yellow-painted noses showed that they belonged to Goering's Luftwaffe elite. But for the protection of the escorting cruisers, Coventry and Dido, and seven destroyers, Aba would have been blown to bits.

Captain A.H. Crapper told how Aba, in spite of wearing her giant red crosses, was deliberately attacked by the Stukas. These dived down to masthead height to unload their deadly "eggs" and to pepper the ship with cannon fire. Every gun in the convoy fought back.

Although badly damaged, Aba remained afloat. Her hull and all her starboard lifeboats were holed, and even some of the rope falls were severed by shrapnel. Incredibly, out of the 630 patients she was carrying, only two were killed. Mortally wounded, the director layer of the Coventry's guns, Warrington-born Petty Officer John

Sephton, carried on the fight. For his great bravery he was awarded the Victoria Cross posthumously.

The war hadn't finished with Aba yet! Helping out in the evacuation of Crete in 1942, she was shelled by shore batteries. Her protector, the Coventry, was sunk a few months later off Tobruk — not to mention other fine ships there, some carrying hundreds of stretcher-cases, which went down with all souls at that grim hot-spot.

For her services in the North Africa campaign, Aba and her commander, Captain Crapper, were cited by General Montgomery in a special order of the day. Under the late Captain E. Brown, Aba continued her war service and was bombed yet again in 1943, while in Naples Bay. This time, three of her patients were killed.

It is not surprising to learn that after the war, Aba was considered unfit to return to her former role of passenger liner. She was sold to the Bawtry Steamship Company and given yet another name — Matrona.

But Glennapp/Aba/Matrona — a heroine by any other name — had her number coming up. As though suffering a heralding stroke, she developed a bad list and overturned while refitting in Bidston Dock on Merseyside. She was refloated and made her last voyage under tow — to the scrapyard, where the breakers did the job that all the bombs had failed to do.

Aba, pictured in the Mersey in the early 1920's.　　(D.P. & E.)

The Matrona (ex-Aba) being winched upright in Bidston Dock, Merseyside.
(D.P. & E.)

Aureol, Accra & Apapa

Last of the Liverpool liners — or rather the last regular big passenger liner to operate from Liverpool — Elder Dempster's 14,000-ton flagship, Aureol, wrote "finis" to the greatest era of Liverpool's maritime history.

The largest Liverpool-West Africa liner in history, she was built by Alexander Stephens and Sons, at Glasgow, and launched on March 28, 1951. She was 537 feet long, with a 70ft. beam, twin screws, oil-fired Doxford engines and had a speed of 16 knots. Aureol could accommodate 253 first-class and 100 cabin passengers, with extra cots for children, and her crew of 209 consisted of European and African personnel.

Although her name was spelt differently, Aureol took this from the famous mountain landmark, Mount Auriol, overlooking Freetown harbour. With her running mates, Accra and Apapa, she was a smart, yacht-like ship, with white hull, buff funnel and buff band and a single tripod mast abaft the bridge, giving her clear visibility and radar vision.

She made her maiden voyage from Liverpool to West Africa on November 8, 1951, on the company's mail and passenger service — coincidentally, perhaps, but also in the centenary year of the start of regular steamship services between Britain and West Africa.

In 1960, Aureol took part in Nigeria's independence celebrations at Lagos, and displayed on her side what was said to have been the largest prefabricated sign (from Liverpool) ever made. This was 80 feet long and 30 feet deep, and depicted the Union Jack and the Nigerian flag.

At Liverpool in 1968, she was involved in a more novel event and probably made a little more history by becoming the venue of an art exhibition for the paintings of scores of sailors from a dozen ships belonging to Ocean Fleet.

Homeward-bound on one of her voyages, she found the 55-years-old vessel, Eppleton Hall, in distress in the notorious Bay of Biscay. Thought to have been the world's last steam paddle-tug, Eppleton Hall had been delayed by bad weather and needed 500 gallons of fuel

---

Overleaf — Top: *The Aureol, last regular passenger liner to sail from the Mersey. Her final voyage from the port wrote the last chapter in the history of the famous liners which sailed from Liverpool.* (D.P. & E.)
Middle: *Elder Dempster flagship, Aureol, at sea. With her sisters, Apapa and Accra, she operated a regular passenger service and a general cargo service between Liverpool and West Africa.* (Ocean Transport and Trading)
Bottom: *The Aureol at Freetown.* (Ocean Transport and Trading)

Above:
Like a lovely white yacht, Aureol poses at anchor in mid-river. (D.P. & E.)

Below:
Accra (III), fresh from her Barrow builders, in September, 1947, was Elder Dempster's first post-war replacement for its passenger fleet.

(F. Strike, Barrow)

Above:
The Accra at Las Palmas.   (Ocean Transport and Trading)

Below:
Awaiting her destiny . . . Accra in Brocklebank Dock, Liverpool, on June 5, 1967, while her future was being discussed.   (D.P. & E.)

Above:
A fine picture of Apapa (III) leaving Brocklebank Dock to start her voyage to West Africa. (D.P. & E.)

Below:
M.V. Apapa basking in the glorious sunshine of Bathurst, Gambia, with some local admirers on the beach. (Ocean Transport and Trading)

Above:
Alongside Prince's Landing Stage, Liverpool, in heavy weather on September 20, 1968, Apapa is making ready for her 177th and last round voyage to West Africa. (Bob Bird, Wallasey)

Below:
Apapa at Liverpool on October 24, 1968 – home for the last time and berthed in Brocklebank Dock on completion of her final voyage to West Africa. She was sold to a Chinese shipping company on November 12 and renamed Taipooshan. (D.P. & E.)

oil in drums. Aureol could not supply this amount of fuel, but stood by the tug until she was taken in tow by a Spanish trawler. The paddle-tug, manned by a volunteer crew, was on passage from the Tyne to San Francisco Maritime Museum.

On September 11, 1971, Aureol left Liverpool with 398 passengers and the company's proud boast: "We haven't had a vacant cabin outward-bound this year." She was, indeed, doing well, when so many passenger liners were fading from the scene. But in November that same year, when Canadian Pacific's Empress of Canada was withdrawn from service, the 20-years-old Aureol found herself to be the last of the regular liners operating from Liverpool.

Her future at Liverpool hung in the balance from thereon, and the company announced: "Keeping the ship running gets more and more expensive as she gets older. Her future must be limited, but how long depends on the circumstances". Those "circumstances" altered quickly, and in March, the following year, it was decided to move Aureol from Liverpool to Southampton. This move was prompted by her replacement on the UK-West African Line's express cargo service from Liverpool to Ghana and Nigeria by a cargo liner, and the forthcoming closure of Prince's Landing Stage passenger facilities at Liverpool.

When she finally bid farewell to Liverpool — her lifetime's home port — on March 16, 1972, with a record number of passengers bound for West Africa, she virtually marked the end of Liverpool's wonderful liner era.

Aureol returned from that voyage to Southampton to start a new 35-day round voyage, in place of the more normal 42-day voyage, calling at Las Palmas, Freetown, Monrovia, Tema and Apapa outwards, and coming home via Takoradi in place of Tema. Among the many famous people carried in this liner were the late President Tubman of Liberia, Dr. Azikiwie, once President of Nigeria, His Highness the Oni of Ife, spiritual leader of the Yeruba People, and Prince William of Gloucester (who, ironically, died in an air crash in August, 1972).

In February, 1974, it was announced that Aureol was to be withdrawn from service that autumn. There had been a gradual decline of passengers on her northwards run and operating costs were high. She was put up for sale in October, and for Elder Dempster it meant the end of a service begun in 1860.

Aureol was to have returned to Merseyside for dry-docking at Birkenhead. Instead, she was diverted to Cornwall's River Fal, where she was laid up until being sold the next month to the Marianna Shipping and Trading Company of Monrovia, which renamed her Marianna IV. The liner was used for ferrying pilgrims to the Saudi-Arabian port of Jedda, the starting point for Mecca.

Aureol outlived the other two of the famous Liverpool trio — sisters, the 11,600-ton Accra and the 11,600-ton Apapa.

Accra, built at Barrow-in-Furness, was launched on February 24, 1947, and made her maiden voyage from Liverpool to West Africa on September 24 that year as the largest post-war passenger liner on that particular service. She was Elder Dempster's first replacement for its passenger fleet, four of which were war casualties. She made 171 round voyages and sailed more than a million miles, carrying 100,000 passengers and 750,000 tons of cargo. On October 11, 1956, she rescued the 77 crew of the 8,472-ton Spanish tanker, Bailen, when their ship caught fire off the Canary Islands.

Accra was withdrawn from service in October, 1967, and on November 8, was sold for demolition at Cartegena, Spain. She sailed

At sea in 1954 . . . Mr. Ernest Willis, of Elder Dempster, lends a helping hand with the children's games on Aureol's promenade deck.

from the Mersey for the last time five days later, under the command of Captain L.L. James.

Apapa, third vessel to bear the name, also built at Barrow and launched on August 18, 1947, made 177 round voyages to the West Coast of Africa from Liverpool, from where she sailed on her maiden voyage on Thursday, March 11, 1948.

During the Queen's and Duke of Edinburgh's visit to Nigeria in 1956, Apapa, berthed at Lagos, was decorated with the Elder Dempster houseflag, a crown and ER II, which were illuminated at night.

On November 12, 1968, Apapa was sold to the Shun-Cheong Steam Navigation Company, of Hong Kong, for further trading, and was renamed Taipooshan. In 1975, she was sold again and scrapped at Taiwan.

The telegraph signals "Stop" as Apapa arrives at Liverpool on completion of her final round voyage on October 24, 1968. On the bridge: Captain Duncan Campbell and Chief Officer Michael Foster. (D.P. & E.)

OTHER TITLES FROM

Local History

Birkenhead Priory	£1.80
The Spire is Rising	£1.95
The Search for Old Wirral	£9.95
Birkenhead Park	£1.40
A Guide to Merseyside's Industrial Past	£1.95
Neston and Parkgate	£2.00
Scotland Road	£5.95
Helen Forrester Walk	£1.00
Women At War	£2.95
Merseyside Moggies	£1.00
Dream Palaces	£7.50
Forgotten Shores	£3.25

Local Shipping Titles

Sail on the Mersey	£1.95
The Mersey at Work — Ferries	£1.40
Ghost Ships on the Mersey	£1.40
The Liners of Liverpool — *Part 1*	£2.95
The Liners of Liverpool — *Part II*	£2.95

Local Railway Titles

Seventeen Stations to Dingle	£2.95
The Line Beneath the Liners	£2.95
Steel Wheels to Deeside	£2.95
Seaport to Seaside	£4.25
Northern Rail Heritage	£1.95
A Portrait of Wirral's Railways	£3.95

History with Humour

The One-Eyed City	£2.95
Hard Knocks	£3.95
The Binmen are Coming	£3.50

Natural History

Birdwatching in Cheshire	£3.95

Other Titles

Speak through the Earthquake, Wind & Fire	£3.95
It's Me, O Lord	£0.40
Companion to the Fylde	£1.75
Country Walks on Merseyside	£1.95